1981

A theory of the classical novel

... le coeur humain dont mon grand-père parlait volontiers en famille, je le trouvais fade et creux partout sauf dans les livres.

SARTRE

A theory of the classical novel

Everett Knight

NEW YORK

BARNES & NOBLE, INC.

Published in the United States of America 1970
by Barnes & Noble, Inc., New York, N.Y.
© *Everett Knight 1970.*

SBN 389 01204 1

Printed in Great Britain

To
Christine
Paul, Peter and Julian

Parts of this book were written during a year's leave from the University of Ghana which I was able to take thanks to a fellowship from the American Council of Learned Societies. I wish to thank the Council for its generosity.

Contents 809.3
K705

98209

1 Some preliminary notions

I'm sure there are many reasons why we study these things
but I missed it due to absence. I brought a note.
Up the Down Staircase

If student agitation persists, and if it manages to organize
itself, we may witness the birth of a new 'social class'—the
world's youth—a 'class' with every right to be concerned about
what is being done on the planet it is going to have to inhabit.

The university campus, like the nineteenth-century mill
village, is the only considerable community in our part of the
world which has not yet been scattered. Here people can be
quickly called together to discuss, decide and, on occasion, show
violence. But while we can understand perfectly how workers
during the last century were driven to rioting and revolution,
we may be puzzled by the students' unhappiness since they are,
in the main, from the material point of view, highly privileged.

The answer, in part, is that the student is informed—informed
of the incredible barbarisms for which *his* culture has made
itself responsible since the turn of the century. He knows that
the present-day working class is to be found in the underdeveloped countries where it is still starving, and he knows
further that the hunger of two-thirds of the world's population
is not an act of God, but of men; that it is directly related to the
way in which *our* western science, economy and military
machine are made to function. In these circumstances student
violence (like that of the American Negroes) is counter-violence,
far more legitimate than the hidden, hypocritical violence of
racism and of the 'impersonal' operation of 'economic law'.

Of course the nineteenth-century student must have had a
fair idea of what conditions were in the factory towns, and if he
did not demonstrate against them it was largely because there
were so many 'higher things' to fix one's mind upon—the moral
law, the iron necessities of a positivistic universe, aestheticism,

1

and so on. But the higher things have all vanished, and where the university teacher tries to interest his students in them he will—or should—meet with mistrust, resentment, boredom.

Until recently the worker was a wage-earner who did not receive a wage sufficient to feed and clothe himself, and his interest in socialism and revolution derived from this immediate daily concern. Such is the case also with the student except that the 'wage' he has a right to expect takes the form not of money but of the means of *making sense of the world he lives in*.[1] However, in exchange for his labour the student is offered on the one hand a mess of facts (either meaningless or confirming what he already knows), on the other, access to the realms of appreciation in a world seething with revolution or sunk in a misery which—since we know now how to abolish it—immemorial religions can no longer satisfactorily explain.

Not only is the student not told how he might make sense of the world and hence of his own life, it is a matter of principle that this should not be done. He is, instead, left free to consider and to judge systems or ideas which have been 'impartially' set before him. The student is given the means, and is encouraged to find out for himself; no one will attempt to push him where he might not want to go. He is free. The opportunity is there if he wishes to take it. What could be more fair?

This is what befuddles the student. He is made to feel like a child rebelling against a kind parent, until one day he is sent to some Vietnam to rain napalm upon people engaged in one of history's great revolutionary ventures. He may then, given the necessary courage, begin to see that he had been closed up within a *specific* political and economic system, that talk of 'pluralism' and of the 'end of ideology' has been a monstrous mystification of which not only the newspapers, but the universities have been guilty. The 'free choice' he had been invited to make on the basis of information 'objectively' submitted to him by his teachers emerges as an aspect of the

---

1 I am referring of course to students in the liberal arts and in the so-called 'sciences of man'. The others—the engineers, physicists, doctors—are the technicians of our society. Their function is clear enough, so that making sense of things is less urgent in their case; they tend consequently to be more conservative in outlook than students in the humanities.

way in which *his* particular society functions. The real choice had already long since been made for him. Let me explain what I mean by the 'real choice'.

A South African government official being interviewed about the nature of the regime he represented tried to make his position clearer by holding up a board which had been divided equally into two parts, one black, one white. The official explained that what they wanted was a society in which neither the black nor the white square would be on top, but one in which they would be on the same level, side by side. Where are we to look for the 'real choice' of the people who support the present South African government; in the words of this official or in the lives of the black part of the population (which should have been symbolized by a square far larger than the white one) ? There can be no doubt about the answer; but then it follows that the real choice of any westerner who is informed but who, unlike some students, does not demonstrate, is to be sought in the eyes of the world's starving. Students learn that western democracy abhors totalitarianism whether Fascist or Communist; but then if they are in the least attentive to events they know that no regime can be too cynically Fascist to sacrifice western support, while talk of land reform or nationalization is a threat to the 'free world'. Where is the real choice; in the immaculate intentions of our western spokesmen, or in their governments' recognition of the Greek democracy recently instituted by a group of moronic colonels?

It is this gulf which has existed in our culture since 1789 between our protestations of liberty, equality and fraternity on the one hand and what we allow to *happen* on the other which makes it impossible for the student or anyone else to *make sense* of our world. And yet if the student has an inalienable right, comparable to the workman's right to a living wage, it is that his teachers be prepared to explain why there is talk of humanism but a practice of racism, talk of the wonders and beauties of Nature along with a systematic defilement of it, talk of sexual freedom and a practice of guilt and frustration, talk of human dignity while the vast majority of the population is condemned to eight hours a day of meaningless wasteful labour. . . .

The inability of our society to accord what it actually does with its noble talk[2] has not (with the exception of Marx and, today, of Sartre) given much concern to philosophers and intellectuals who have in general devoted themselves to the pursuit of one or another of the higher things, leaving the messier questions to novelists.

It is in the novel[3] that our culture has most consistently and profoundly examined itself: why then should we not use it in somewhat the way a psychoanalyst uses the talk of a patient, to get at what I have been calling the real choice, a choice to which the patient may cling even though it is keeping him from making any sense of his life, even though it could lead him to suicide?

It is important to mention some of the difficulties not of executing such a project, but merely of attempting to do so.

One may not be able to follow an argument for one of two radically different reasons. First, because what is being discussed is beyond one's competence: present-day atomic physics, for example, cannot be *really* grasped without long and arduous preparation. The second difficulty is one which arises rarely, only at times (like our own) of profound cultural reorientation, and it consists in not seeing the relevance of the

2 This problem exists perhaps in all cultures, but in ours it is crucial because noble talk is an alibi, it is *part* of the crime inasmuch as we all know that man is 'alone', that there is *only* humanity, and that therefore we are responsible. The mediaeval robber barons ignored the moral teaching of the Church, but they were also accounted for by it in terms of the 'fall of man' and various other theological notions; or, to express this differently, in all primitive societies political authority cannot be entirely disengaged from the sacred. But there is no accounting for Nazi crimes except in Sartrean terms (which we indignantly reject) of the *choice* of evil on the part of a few and the *choice* of acquiescence (however reluctant) on the part of the rest of us. There was no place in bourgeois ideology for the brutality of the factory system except through recourse to economic 'law'; but how could this be done in good faith in a century of revolution? And then also, every historical period has perhaps what Sartre calls a *tiers régulateur*, a man who is ignored or persecuted not because he offends reason and morality, but because he announces the incontrovertible; because he makes public what is already known, in however 'unexplicated' a form, in private.

3 By the 'classical novel' I mean that written between the end of the picaresque and the inauguration by Kafka of the contemporary novel. We will return to this of course; in the meantime, by 'novel' I mean the classical novel.

ideas being presented. Thus Galileo's physics were not difficult in the first, but in the second sense of the word, for the schoolmen of the time. They simply could not see the interest or importance of what Galileo was doing. It is like trying to pronounce the sounds of a foreign tongue; they are not difficult 'in themselves', but only because our mouths have through long practice become so formed that only our own vowel system comes 'naturally'. The difficulty is not so much acquiring the new as getting rid of the old.

What the scholastics must have found disconcerting was the fact that the early scientists were not proposing a new body of truths, but, essentially, a *method for arriving at the truth*. That the earth should revolve around the sun rather than the reverse, was less important in itself than for what it was hoped this discovery would lead to, and the work of Newton seemed to confirm once and for all the validity of this startling notion of a truth arrived at only *progressively*.

If progress were to be uninterrupted then men would have to accept the discipline of remaining uncommitted to any conclusion not scientifically verified. Such has been the 'morality' of the western intellectuals to the present day: a kind of 'waiting' associated with an objective, dispassionate gathering of information (the facts) insignificant and meaningless at the moment perhaps, but destined to be needed for the great Tabulation, the reward of centuries of patient waiting. In his *Discours de la Méthode*, Descartes announced that he intended to abide by the laws and customs of his country until such time as science could pronounce definitively upon these matters. We are still waiting, but of course the 'laws and customs' have not waited. On the first page of J. K. Galbraith's book *The Great Crash—1929* there occurs this sentence: 'It would be good to know if we shall someday have another 1929. However, the much less pretentious task of this book—the only task which social science in its present state allows—is to tell what happened in 1929.' Who will be so pretentious as to decide when all the information is in? Such a moment cannot coincide with the discovery of a 'natural law', since we would then have to decide what action to take in respect to it, and this of course is incompatible with the notion of natural law. Would it be wise to wait, if not for the great Tabulation,

5

then at least until we know more? But while we are waiting the nature of the problems will have changed, and quite apart from any will of ours. In brief, in the century of the Russian, Chinese, Cuban and Vietnamese revolutions, in a century which has demonstrated so conclusively that man's fate is one he alone determines, we in the West are waiting for the scientific millennium, waiting for Godot.

We are at one of those exceptional moments in history during which long-standing mental attitudes produce a reality which, with another part of our being we are obliged to find absurd or horrifying. The schoolmen Rabelais made fun of must have known, however obscurely, that they were survivors, pathetically trying to cope with what we have come to call the Age of Discovery, pathetically mistaking one reality for another. In the same way, in our Age of Revolution it is possible for an 'illustrious representative of logical positivism' to maintain that: 'A knowledge of chemistry is more important to a philosopher than a knowledge of history'.[4] One need not be familiar with the development of contemporary thought from Hegel to Sartre to feel compassion for a 'philosopher' given to such remarks. But when one considers that we are dealing here less with a philosophy than with what I called a moment ago a 'mental attitude', compassion turns justifiably into something like hatred; for when a political scientist or sociologist goes to, say, Guatemala to research into conditions there, and when he notes *objectively* the existence of starving children, he treats his fellow creatures as the chemist dispassionately treats the substances he investigates in his laboratory; he becomes a cultural freak, not comic as were the schoolmen for Rabelais, but sinister. In chemistry one makes discoveries; but when the sociologists, after long investigation, announce that Negro rioting in America is caused by white racism, they discover what everyone already knows; so that what needs investigation is the investigators themselves. The Negroes, after long patience, are meeting violence with counter-violence. This requires no explanation, they are performing a task which has been forced not only

4 See Alphonse de Waelhens's *La Philosophie et les Expériences Naturelles*, Nijhoff, La Haye, p. 77.

upon them, but upon all of us; except, of course, in so far as we can persuade ourselves that impartial recording of the facts is all that 'social science in its present state allows'. In short, what needs to be investigated, because it is irrational, is that 'mental attitude' which transforms a self-evident task, a summons, into the dead matter which is the domain of the physical sciences. Such conduct can be understood only if we assume that the logical positivist, the social scientist, the literary historian, the English-speaking intelligentsia almost in its entirety is waiting for the discovery of a Given in which, nevertheless, no one any longer believes! The 'scientific waiting' of the eighteenth century which was in part scepticism and tolerance, has become the calculated apathy of a privileged class.

It is difficult to see how anyone today could seriously reject the view that philosophy and the history of philosophy are one and the same thing; that philosophy in other words is not after an elusive Truth which, hopefully, it will one day attain. It follows then that philosophy is an aspect of those 'mental attitudes' which, as was said a moment ago, *produce* a reality which is nevertheless *out there* and can be profitably investigated (just as a literary masterpiece is the 'product' of a given mentality, yet susceptible to diverse interpretations, each valid as far as it goes). So that however dull and dangerous the reality produced by Anglo-Saxon positivism, it is there, and it is not always easy to adjust our vision to new possibilities. And yet although Galileo and Descartes were 'irresponsible adventurers' in the sense that their reality was not yet visible, there was no alternative. The scholastics did not essentially choose for sound reasons to ignore science, they ignored the times they lived in. It is the same with today's intellectuals trying to deal with twentieth-century reality with nineteenth-century vision, one of the most important manifestations of which was the omniscience of the nineteenth-century novelist. We know that this omniscience (or the objectivity of the scholar, or the fixed point of view of the classical artist) does not capture Reality, it indistinguishably produces and reveals a specific reality, that characteristic of western culture during a certain stage of its evolution. Yet the knowledge that we are culturally and historically situated, that positivism is a metaphysic like any other, does not shake the conviction that we are 'non-committed'; so that whether it is an American soldier fighting to enable the Vietnamese to 'freely choose their own government', or a scholar telling me this book is 'personal and polemic', we encounter this strange objective vantage point which is somehow not a particular point of view, but one from which all other conceivable points of view may be judged (a striking example of the ethnocentrism we find so amusing in primitive people).

It is true that this book is a personal one; the result of discovering that I was passing my life as a teacher with absolutely nothing to teach. I was therefore compelled to somehow *make sense* of the matter I was placed in charge of. The alternative is an impersonality which, naturally, augments in proportion as the teacher ceases to be a person so as to purvey with more machine-like efficiency those facts for which the student will be held responsible at examination time and which he could almost as easily have found in the library for himself. There are perhaps two generally accepted ways in which the teacher can do a little more without falling into some 'commitment' and so disqualifying himself:[5] he can teach the student to appreciate what to the mind of the layman is utterly unappreciable, so that a student who reads passionately the *Faerie Queene* or *Clarissa Harlowe* belongs to a tiny élite which, by separating the aesthetic from the vital human problems of the moment, condemns 'beauty' to the learned journals. Secondly, the teacher might, if he is sufficiently gifted and erudite, take up and explain what is most relevant for us in the work of history's great thinkers and writers; but this brings us back to the difficulty already mentioned: the times are such that the only really relevant thinking is one that gives us a perspective upon the myth of non-involvement; one that is a choice and a programme; one which, consequently, if taught 'objectively' is by that very fact rejected. Again the

5 The teacher is of course always free to be a partisan of anything he likes provided it does not offer a practical alternative to existing social and political conditions; in fact, this sort of idiosyncrasy (being a Zen Buddhist for example) is encouraged as a substitute for the genuine individualism the university is said to foster.

8

Renaissance parallel is useful: in the seventeenth century educated men were either fascinated by the new 'scientific vision' or they remained futilely preoccupied with the debris of the Aristotelian-Christian universe.

Everyone, then, is 'personal and polemic', only the goals differ. If our personal commitment is to a group sufficiently large and influential (like the academic community) we can pretend it does not exist, for the goal is already attained; numbers have prevailed.

Revolutions do not come about because conditions are intolerable but because, in the light of new conceptions, men become aware they are intolerable. Similarly with philosophies, the old do not simply become absurd (like positivism waiting for the emerging of an Order in which no one any longer believes), they have to be undermined and replaced; so that in what has been written so far I have taken for granted that cultures exist as structured wholes. I have also taken for granted that these 'totalities' (to use Sartre's expression) build up as a consequence of human enterprise in all its forms, and are fully comprehensible in these terms. This is the reason for my use of such bizarre and unscholarly expressions as 'real choice' and 'to make sense of'. I have been trying to make sense of nineteenth- and twentieth-century positivism not only because it dominates approaches to the history of literature but also as a useful preliminary to making sense of the classical novel. It would appear that the 'objective waiting' of the positivist (that is, of most western academics) presupposes the existence of a Meaning, an Order, of a given,[6] in brief, independent of the 'human enterprise' just referred to; so that positivism, in common with all past systems of thought and

6 By the word 'positivism' I mean, as already mentioned, not only the philosophy, but the entire cultural orientation of western (and in particular English-speaking) civilization. In his *Art et Technique aux 19e et 20e siècles*, for example, Pierre Francastel shows how most contemporary thinking about art is made obsolescent by a continual and often no doubt only half-conscious positing of a given: the 'real world', 'Nature', the 'organic', and so forth. The creation of a 'universe-object' which man confronts as subject was one of the great and necessary achievements of early science; it is now an increasingly dangerous obstacle to understanding the times we live in.

religion, seeks to account for the human in terms of the non-human. The positivist does not help matters by pointing out that he seeks merely to 'save the appearances'. Koestler, for example, in *The Sleepwalkers*, rebukes Galileo for not regarding science as simply a more satisfactory means of 'saving the appearances' rather than absolute truth at last within reach. This is to criticize Galileo for having lived in the seventeenth century when the intellectual excitement of the time consisted precisely in the belief that it would now be possible to go beyond the saving of appearances. Had Galileo been more gifted he might have been able, like the positivist of today (more interested in chemistry than in history), to be born into no particular century but rather into that objective olympian place from which the whole sorry history of man can be viewed as the fanatical pursuit of one non-existent truth after the other. It is never easy to live in one's own time, and to do so now it is not sufficient to reinforce Hume's scepticism with the total disillusionment of a third-rate thinker like Camus so as to produce an ever loftier objectivity. Performing the miracle of objectivity, with or without despair, is no longer arduous; it is far more difficult to be a 'fanatic' like Galileo, to be attached to the truth of our time of which talk of the 'absurd' is the negative aspect serving only to clear away what Sartre calls 'theological thinking': that directed toward the discovery of a given, the existence of which, consequently, will be *fully* intelligible only to God. Fortunately, however, there is no given. The appearances which the positivist saves are appearances of his choice, and to save them 'positivistically', is only one way of accounting for them. The positivist's choice is justified only in so far as it is 'sustained' by a vast and complex cultural structure seeking its coherence primarily in the direction of measurement and quantity.

A place for the classical novel must somehow be found within that coherence. How can the novel be studied with no reference to the society which produced it?, and yet how many 'structural' studies of the novel exist? Again we are confronted by that strange combination of what is manifestly absurd—the part (both the novel and the novelist himself) analysed out of its context and 'researched' into, in much the way the chemist isolates and purifies substances in the laboratory—along with the half inability, half refusal to do something about it. Half refusal because, as Marx says, men do not set themselves problems they cannot solve; and the 'solution' to the inanities of a moribund positivism is the new rationality which has been developing from Hegel through Marx, Husserl, Freud and Heidegger to Sartre.

Thinking which does not have woven into it an awareness of global problems condemns itself on that ground alone; and from a global point of view, we live in an age of unprecedented political, cultural, economic, and technological revolution. What this means, essentially, is that for ever-increasing numbers of men reality is purely and simply the 'raw material' which humanity adapts to its needs. In our part of the world the largest single body of people who realize this, in however disorganized and inarticulate a manner, is the students; but they have the misfortune to be dependent upon an institution which, more or less hypocritically, continues to regard reality as a given. The result—again from a global point of view— is a widening gap between our ideology (liberty, equality, fraternity) and the Real, between what we say and what we actually do; and in so far as the university considers its function to be that of investigating the nature of the Real while contenting itself in times of crisis with saying the right things, then the university is an almost indispensable bulwark of the system as it exists; for if the Real is susceptible *only* to one form or another of 'contemplation', the expression of the finest sentiments and wishes is all that can be required of anyone.

There is no Real independent of the manner in which we take cognizance of it; so that the 'objective waiting' of the western intellectual has created our preposterous world of the significantless fact. If, consequently, we are ever again to make sense of things, what we must interrogate is not the real 'in itself' (which does not exist) but the whole cultural orientation which insists that this is the Real and not that.

In this light, we can appreciate the difficulties less of finding out what structural role the novel may play in our culture than of persuading publishers and their academic consultants that it is time such an attempt were made.[7] For if we are to

11

understand the novel we begin necessarily by rejecting the approach which makes it unintelligible: 'objective waiting' and its correlate in the real, the significantless fact. But if we do so—and this is how the system perpetuates itself—we fall automatically into the 'personal and polemical' on the one hand, and we are 'off the subject' on the other.

The novel is not a fact, it is a comportment; a comportment which (like all human activity) is not caused, it is inspired by self-appointed goals (some of which may not be fully conscious) which we either share or disapprove of, since to be 'objective' is to approve by default. In studying the novel we are therefore, of necessity, personal. But also the 'goals' of the novel will make little sense except by reference to the culture as a whole; we will therefore be, and again by necessity, 'off the subject' as far as the specialist is concerned—a specialist being one versed in a particular area and time-segment of significantless fact.

If the Real is the consequence so to speak of a 'fusion' between a particular cultural vision and whatever it is in the nature of that vision to 'highlight' or to 'elicit' from the 'raw material' (Sartre's *en-soi*) of the universe, then we advance in wisdom and knowledge not by penetrating to that deep-hidden ultimate law which was the goal of nineteenth-century scientism, but by adopting a vision which will embrace more, which can encompass the new and awkward phenomena which historical change keeps thrusting upon our awareness. Scholasticism could not for long coexist with men and ships capable of circumnavigating the globe. What was needed in the age of the voyages of discovery and of the new infinite universe was a philosophy which, if it were to be sufficiently universal,

---

7 Hence the publication of this book will have been delayed for many years. I am in the position of a Marxist economist trying to make himself heard by people who talk of marginal utility, supply and demand, and the like. These concepts are useful for just as long as you can accept the system *as it is* and are content to work *within it*. But then, to have the courage of such a system, one would have to admire the exemplary W. W. Rostow, the Harvard professor of economics turned State Department war-lord, intent upon bombing the North Vietnamese back into the Stone Age because they refuse to wait—like the obliging, starving Indians—for the 'take-off' point of their economy to be reached.

could be based only upon measure and quantity. But now this philosophy in its turn leaves out too much; it leaves out nothing less than time, or at least time as *qualitative change*. It leaves us unable, in other words, to deal with what has been, since the French Revolution, the most conspicuous aspect of western life. It leaves us the impotent (i.e. the scientific, objective) observers of processes which, in the light of philosophy since Hegel, it has become impossible to attribute to anything but one form or another of human initiative. The purpose of Husserl's *Die Krisis der Europaischen Wissenschaften* is to show that science itself is such an 'initiative' (or 'comportment', as I have just said of the novel). That which comes first in any system of inquiry is not the results, but those presuppositions which cause only results of this nature to be considered fully satisfactory, all others being dismissed as irrelevant. A given structure of presupposition is at once indispensable—for there to be any knowledge at all it has to be that of an historically situated culture—and yet in a very real sense it is a choice, an initiative. What complicates matters is that these choices can be at one extreme almost totally opaque (structure of language, Freudian unconscious) and at the other they can be flagrant examples of bad faith, as when we presuppose the 'necessity' of doing precisely what we wanted most to do. This will be one of our most delicate problems: to determine the measure of 'unconsciousness' in the classical novelist's choice of reality.

We have seen that the objective approach to reality produces a distorted reality which, nevertheless, the intellectual will generally prefer to look upon as the whole of the Real, all else being 'subjective' and/or 'not to the point'.[8] This constitutes

8 Think, for example, of a sociologist interviewing a Detroit automobile worker and learning that the man is, by and large, satisfied with his job since (assuming this to be the case) wages are high and employment secure. What the interviewer would not see, since this sort of thing is 'subjective' and 'irrelevant', is the appalling vacuity of expression in the worker's face, a consequence of his being excluded for life from any decision-making function in his society. Nothing could be more visible than this deadness of expression which has become the expression of the North American face, yet it must remain invisible (except, of course, for art and literature which has nothing to do with what the positivist regards as essential to truth) because it is not significantless, it is not measurable.

a major difficulty in my trying to make sense of the novel in terms of what the novelist (and his society) may mean by adopting such a form of expression; in terms of those goals which, half-consciously, half-unaware, are being pursued through nineteenth-century fiction and in our own time through many forms of mass 'entertainment'. In more general terms, the difficulty is this: how is one to render a theory of the novel convincing for English-speaking readers without dwelling at length upon the great reorientation of contemporary philosophy which makes an attempt to formulate such a theory both natural and opportune? Since Marx's contribution to the 'new rationality' has been decisive, how is one to write anything of consequence today which will not by implication at least incriminate that provincialism of Anglo-Saxon philosophy which is an aspect of the deep and disastrous conservatism of our political philosophy?

I cannot abandon my attempt to make sense of the novel since then, as I mentioned a moment ago, there would be nothing for me to teach; and yet the importance of the results arrived at will be missed if they are assumed to be those of an individual enterprise rather than one of the consequences of a vast collective effort to alter the foundations of western thought. For anyone writing in English there is of course no solution at the moment to this dilemma since, as we saw, to offer an 'objective' account of the ideas of men like Marx and Sartre is the surest indication we have failed to understand them; for such an account is first of all a specific initiative the purpose and nature of which, conveniently, will form no part of the inquiry.[9]

I should like to continue to 'circle' for a moment in this way, exploring a little further some of the implications of the two basic notions—praxis (initiative) and structure—I have been using from the beginning. It is natural there should be no 'linear argument' where the purpose of the argument is to call into question the traditional points of reference, and where the

9 If it did, we would be forced to Sartre's conclusion that 'analytical reason', when it comes to historical and social questions, is a 'praxis of oppression'. (*Critique de la Raison Dialectique*, Gallimard, 1960, p. 743.)

subject cannot and yet must be treated so briefly. We will be able to progress in a somewhat 'straighter line' when we reach the novel.

Both these conceptions (and for a rapidly changing society like our own one should perhaps say praxis-structure-alienation) we owe primarily to Marx and to him also we owe what is equally important—the lesson that the two cannot be dissociated;[10] which implies that, in the final analysis, structure is something men have done, it is 'congealed praxis'. This being the case, Marxism is the first philosophy to have built into it the requirement of self-interrogation. Since Marxism regards the various human cultures as being fundamentally the delicate and complex means by which men carry on what Sartre calls the 'struggle against scarcity', Marxism is obliged to account for itself in these same terms. In other words, since Marxism, properly understood, represents a sweeping away of most of the traditional premises of western thought, to be legitimate it must have been conceived at a moment when the conditions of man's struggle against scarcity were being drastically modified; and it must, in addition, offer the only means we have of dealing effectively with these changes. Does Marxism have this legitimacy?

It would seem that by the 1840s it had become possible, at least for a man of genius like Marx, to see that for the first time in human history, thanks to the agricultural and industrial revolutions, *men were beginning to adapt their environment to themselves rather than having to adapt themselves to their environment.* Egypt could be used as a simple illustration: the relative success of ancient Egyptian civilization was due to the existence in the Nile Valley of natural conditions so favourable that it was possible, regularly, to produce an agricultural surplus. However elaborate and extensive Egyptian systems of irrigation may have been, we can hold that they represented a skilful

10 I mention this because it happens too commonly. Structuralists like Lévi-Strauss and Michel Foucault are creating a sort of neo-positivism which, like the old, enables the scholar to forget that knowing is a form of doing, a form of praxis which, by seeking only fixity, not only 'discovers' it, but condemns us to it. Inversely, praxis 'alone' is deflected and mystified by the structures it does not have the patience to understand, as with Camus's 'revolt' and, at the moment at least, student unrest. It is part of Sartre's greatness that, like Marx, he keeps a balance.

utilization rather than an *alteration* of nature,[11] since a river delta is in itself a 'natural' system of irrigation. The construction of the Assuan Dam, on the other hand, will alter natural conditions; the formation of a huge lake will create a new region with a somewhat different climate, wildlife and vegetation. It is no longer unimaginable that man should one day alter 'nature' to the point of suppressing it altogether—by destroying life or by moving it to another planet.

And yet as human praxis draws near to omnipotence, individual people feel their freedom and responsibility diminishing in proportion. They are increasingly alienated in a world which, increasingly, they can see to be man made.

There can be little hesitation in accepting this as the problem upon which all the others depend: why does man's helplessness increase with his power to alter the environment? How are we to guarantee that men will be free to use their tools and products rather than being used by them?

Marxism then comes at a moment of qualitative change in conditions of life on this planet, and to bring about a comparable change in our habits of thought, we must see that science, structural or otherwise, is a philosophy, not a vantage point from which all other manner of thought may be dismissed as metaphysical for refusing to wait. The soundness of a system of thought, in other words, can no longer be 'internal'; it can be based neither upon 'discovery' (science) nor revelation (religion) nor coherence (logic, dogmatic structuralism). Such thinking is 'internal' in the sense that it feeds back into itself; the new becomes increasingly what we are condemned to *live*, more or less blindly, while thought is most at its ease in domains as remote as possible from daily existence. A few years ago I crossed the Sahara in a jet 30,000 feet up. At five o'clock a Moslem passenger went to the front of the plane, spread his prayer mat and knelt facing east. It is not only for Islam, however, that change as startling as that from camel to air

11 As Marx points out in the *Theses on Feuerbach* and elsewhere, there is no nature in the abstract, but only nature 'worked upon' by men (or, as we would say, 'constituted' by men—this being the theme of Sartre's *La Nausée*). But while changes brought about by modern technology are, in a sense, changes in degree only, they are so radical that we can safely regard them as being changes in kind as well.

16

transport is an illusion. For science also, in so far as it is causal (or, today, narrowly structural), change is necessarily illusory, for if the new were not already present in its cause it would be inexplicable. (In the classical novel, as we shall see, time is not change, but a gradual confirmation of the already given.)

Yet how can we accept the *reality* of change, how can we give the new its full value, without depriving ourselves of the means of thinking it? If we attempt to force the new into traditional forms it will destroy us as it has destroyed primitive societies all over the world; but to refuse to organize the new is to organize chaos, to become arbitrary and directionless. Sartre put it this way: 'I believe that what we need is an evolving truth, and yet a certainty as well so we can judge'. In other words, if we realize that thought is not contact with 'an instantaneous' [what I have been calling a given] but with 'a reality having a past and a future, then a temporal truth becomes possible, one which will often be probable, but sometimes apodictic and therefore not dependent upon the totality of history or upon the sciences'.[12] Sartre was later to find in Marxism a philosophy dependent neither upon the totality of history nor upon the sciences; but it was also a philosophy which had succumbed, after Marx, to positivist facility—it had transformed history into a natural process; so that it is not man, but nature which is 'dialectical'.[13] Once again, in accord with philosophical practice in our part of the world since the Renaissance, the thinker takes an initiative which he is compelled to ignore; he places historical change 'in exteriority' and then discovers it there, rather in the way the nineteenth-century capitalist discovered—much to his advantage—the iron laws of economics. The 'advantages' which accrue to the pre-Marxist intellectual upon his identifying a totally other in respect to which he is, miraculously, unsituated, are those for which we all hunger: for the militant, automatic and infallible response to the new—what Lukacs

12 *Conscience de Soi et Connaissance de Soi*, Bulletin de la Société Française de Philosophie, 42e année, No. 3, Avril-Juin 1948, pp. 80–81.

13 See *Marxisme et Existentialisme: Controverse sur la Dialectique* (Sartre, Garaudy, Hyppolite, etc.) Plon, 1962; and *Critique de la Raison Dialectique*, pp. 115–135.

called a 'volitional idealism'; for others, the comfort and innocence of objective waiting.

If we accept that discovery (whether of the 'instantaneous' or of the 'dialectic of nature') and waiting for discovery are in the last analysis initiatives, praxes, then we clear away substantial obstacles to a clear-sighted appreciation of the new. But then do we not confront it defenceless, guideless? Where is the 'certainty' Sartre refers to above, the apodictic, or self-evident?

Marx's *Capital* is a structural study of our society. A study not intended to establish the 'eternal laws' of history and economics, but to enable us to understand how a specific system operates. We are being told, consequently, not how the system will evolve of itself in accord with natural law, but how we can make it evolve. We are being made acquainted not with fixed truths (which do not exist), but with truths which, being local and transitory in nature, are 'temporal truths'. We have seen that scientific reasoning lacks a solid foundation because what we 'discover' depends upon the questions we put, and positivism avoids putting the indispensable question of the nature of its particular questions. The main purpose of Sartre's *Critique de la Raison Dialectique* is to establish the legitimacy of dialectical reasoning in this respect; to guarantee, in other words, the validity of the method Marx uses in *Capital*, and he does this by demonstrating that we never encounter phenomena not determined essentially by some implicit or explicit human project.[14] The question 'What is this?' cannot be answered except in so far as it is preceded by the question 'How and why did we—or they—bring this about?'

If the world is entirely and exclusively human, if there can be no significance which does not have its origin in human praxis, then the truth must be what, in one form or another, we already know; it may often be 'masked' but it is none the less part of the 'permanent experience of each one of us'.[15]

14 One can hardly read the *Critique* and miss this, but pages 247 and 248 are particularly important for this question.

15 *Critique*, p. 132. What is self-evident in existence is not what we should move *toward* (since there are no Answers) but *away from*. Sartre puts it this way: 'What we want today is simply the hidden other side of what we do

Scientific truth, on the contrary, is no one's experience[16] because, being 'universal', it is necessarily accord upon an absolute minimum (measurement) so that: '. . . the object of agreement becomes exterior to each'.[17] What matters in the life of each of us is put aside while the waiting proceeds; the exigence of total clarity leaves us in almost total ignorance as far as daily experience is concerned.

If, as Sartre repeats, 'all is praxis', and if, consequently, the object of history (and of philosophy) is to 'understand what we know',[18] if the truth, defined as the possible, defined as the action which these circumstances call for, is always in theory accessible to us, then the only obstacle to a reasonably successful adaptation of the environment to man, is man himself.

The argument, it will be remembered, is that the agricultural and industrial revolutions of the eighteenth and nineteenth centuries are a watershed in the history of man in that they are making of us the absolute masters of the natural environment; and to face such a challenge we need a philosophy enabling us to think the radically new (the result of rapid technological development) and at the same time live it; that is, keep it from acquiring that crazy autonomy which makes men the victims of their own achievements. We need a philosophy in others words for which doing and thinking is one and the same, for which the 'exterior world' is simply the seizing into the inert of apraxis which *is* the 'inner world', which therefore is not entity (as for the classical novel notably) but initiative.

What we have arrived at is this: 'Men make history on the basis of the conditions in which they find themselves';[19] and this process tends to circularity because: '. . . men are 'mediated' by things to the degree in which things are

---

not want' (quoted by Francis Jeanson in *Sartre*, Desclée de Brouwer, 1966, p. 137); and Merleau-Ponty thinks along the same lines when he sees in Marxism an attempt to 'eliminate the irrational' in history (*Eloge de la Philosophie et Autres Essais*, Gallimard, 1960, p. 59.)

16 *Critique*, p. 124. 18 *Critique*, p. 107.
17 *Critique*, p. 527. 19 *Critique*, p. 131.

"mediated" by men'.[20] Men 'make history', which is to say that they set themselves goals which can only be attained by 'mediating things'; but then these things acquire exigencies of their own (the tool not only serves, it has *to be* served) they become what Sartre calls the *pratico-inerte*: matter which, having 'absorbed' praxis takes on a borrowed life to create new conditions on the basis of which new goals must be set.

Literature and art are aspects of this 'dialectical circularity', so that two questions will have to be put to the novel: what is it about; what sense can be made of it in terms of the goals men may be attempting to attain through it; and secondly, does this praxis 'congeal' into a structure in such a way that the novel becomes 'unwieldy', bringing about an element of 'alienation' for some authors (Zola, possibly) until finally the structure, having become intolerable, is broken (Kafka)?[21]

There is a third question implied by the other two: any structure in fiction we may succeed in isolating will have to 'fit into' a more comprehensive structure which, since we are dealing with *our* society, will be that of the economy. This recurrence of structure—if we can establish it—in different registers, a consequence of the same fundamental 'project' being pursued at different levels by different means, will serve to reassure us as to the validity of the results arrived at.

But demonstration by homology (to borrow Lucien Goldmann's term) cannot be enough, because then it will be said that we have simply found what we were looking for. In other words we expose ourselves to the same criticism we have made of the positivists: that of failing to inquire into the nature of our questions. Just as we have accused the positivists of finding nothing because they seek nothing,[22] they will

---

20 *Critique*, p. 165.

21 We find, as one would expect, the same evolution in art. Between the Renaissance and Cézanne perspective was the foundation of western art. During that period there could be no *great* art which ignored this particular method of presenting the real. By the end of the last century, inversely, there could be no genuinely great art for which perspective did not distort and impoverish the real.

22 It must often be difficult, nevertheless, even for the logical positivist to find nothing. In *Les Mandarins* Simone de Beauvoir's heroine discovers that indifference (waiting) is not a practicable attitude in life. By continually slipping into indignation or disgust she was, despite herself, affirming

accuse us of finding only what we have placed there out of some dark and twisted motivation. Scholarship, like everything else, is a praxis; which means that it has to be self-interrogating. It is not sufficient that the facts be scrupulously respected, we must give reasons for having taken up a position such that these facts are thrown into relief while others recede into insignificance. If the questions we put lead us to important discoveries then this is, to be sure, an encouraging sign; and yet we know that scientific questions have led to 'answers' which could destroy us. How is the vantage point we adopt to be chosen, since there is no objectivity in the traditional sense?

We saw in the preceding section that not only does the conduct of life not require the discovery of, or the waiting for, the extra-human, our whole problem is to rid ourselves of this spectre so as to be able to see that praxis is its own guide, its own 'light'; that there exist apodictic truths taking the form of universally acknowledged goals which our society has set for itself. We have here the means of simultaneously thinking and living the new; to think effectively we need a *distance which is not a separation*, and we can achieve this by placing ourselves in the future by embracing those goals about which (apart from bad faith, mystification, ignorance and so forth) there is very general agreement. Only from such a vantage point will progress in the 'sciences of man' be possible. Let us take the work of Marx as an example of this notion of 'creative awareness'.[23]

One can hardly read a page of Marx without encountering his anger that there should be men glad to condemn the great majority of their fellows to the appalling conditions in which the nineteenth-century proletariat had to live; and yet simultaneously we are not allowed to forget that industry is a great and necessary stage in human development.

---

that: '. . . this world is full of things to love or to hate . . .', and '. . . it was due to fatigue, laziness and shame of her ignorance' that she had tried to believe otherwise (Gallimard, 1954, p. 343).

23 'His science [that of Marx] is not only a science of social reality; it contributes to the creation of that reality by the manner in which it becomes conscious of it; or at least, it modifies it in depth . . .'. (Jean Hyppolite, *Bulletin de la Société Française de Philosophie*, 42 année, No. 6, October–December 1948, p. 179).

Not only must we stop supposing that this is 'contradictory', we must learn to see that the apparent contradiction is the source of the *scientific* value of Marx's work. For industry is *pratico-inerte;* it has a 'borrowed life' (the 'economic laws' of orthodox economists) which has to be 'sustained' by those who own the means of production, by those whose praxis it is to infuse life into the economic machine which would otherwise remain 'inert'. Yet the 'animation' communicated to the inert in this manner is real (and therefore amenable to scientific inquiry); sufficiently real for many a fortune to have been lost in periods of economic depression. But since the movement of the economy is, in the final analysis, that of a praxis, there is no hope of understanding it scientifically in the positivist acceptation of the word; that is, by presupposing a radical separation between observer and observed and then failing to remark that an initiative has been taken which will deeply affect the nature of the observed. The only genuine 'objectivity' will have to be that of a praxis aware of itself as such and differing from that under investigation. What Marx did, therefore, was to use as a point of departure those truths which derive from the praxis of our society *as a whole* (as opposed to that of a class—the bourgeoisie) and which are, by and large, those we associate with the eighteenth century, with the *revolutionary phase* of the development of our culture. This ideology—liberty, equality, fraternity—represents an 'historical subjectivity'; but for that very reason it is self-evident (as is, for the individual, a love or a hate) so that when Marx begins with the statement that it is intolerable people should live and work in *these* conditions, he begins with the indubitable; with a 'subjective' awareness which is a *condition of the revelation of the real* and not an obstacle to it. We can show how this works by discussing one of the great acquisitions of Marx's structural analysis of capitalism.

If our own age is essentially that during which men became capable of altering the environment rather than having to 'alter' themselves (as in stoicism, mysticism, the 'psychosomatic' feats of primitive peoples, psychoanalysis in so far as it proposes to adapt the individual to the very society which is driving him crazy . . .) then the eighteenth century will be revolutionary precisely to the extent in which it liberated men from the feudal hierarchical order so they might be absorbed into a 'universal' cycle of production. Hence such notions as freedom, equality, reason, and the pre-Marxist version of the labour theory of value which helped prepare people's minds for life in a far more mundane society, one in which *everyone* could be expected to contribute to the *common* good by engaging in some socially useful activity.

But with the full development of the factory system there came into being what Merleau-Ponty called: '. . . the paradox of a society of exploitation founded nevertheless upon the recognition of one man by another'[24] (that is, upon equality; the nobleman did not 'recognize' the serf as a fellow human being). The question then is what happened to the enlightenment's declaration of our common humanity? How, for example, could an expression like 'the dignity of labour', which might have been used with reasonable honesty in 1750 have become a century later one of the vilest of the many middle-class hypocrisies? Why should the community of interests of 'masters and men' which was real in the eighteenth century, since it was to the advantage of both that feudalism be destroyed, have become the famous imbecility: 'What is good for General Motors is good for America'? Why should it have been necessary for the indubitable and universal awareness of our common humanity to have been obscured by every possible means (one of them, as we shall see, being the novel) to such an extent that, as Stendhal remarked, the most notable characteristic of our society is its hypocrisy?

Marx answers by pointing out that, as the number of people brought into the towns and factories increased, the point was reached where one could talk of the *socialization* of labour, while on the other hand there was no corresponding change in ownership of the means of production which remained *individual*.

This contradiction came into being by a process no one deliberately intended. It is consequently 'out there', it can be observed and studied, but only by avoiding the non-existent 'objective' point of view. It is 'brought into focus' in proportion as we espouse unconditionally a certain number of

24 *Les Aventures de la Dialectique*, Gallimard, 1955, p. 54.

apodictic truths which owe their self-evidence to the fact that the material means of realizing certain possibilities clearly exist; or, to put this in another way, our common humanity owes its evidence to men having become the masters of their history (the last generalized famine in France took place in 1709) except in so far as other men (and not God, not scientific law) enslave and mystify them.

We can appreciate now the way in which Marx breaks down the rigid separation positivism has always tried to maintain between 'ought' and 'is'. From what has been said, for instance, it follows that common ownership of the means of production, if productive capacities are not to be cramped or wasted, is at once 'necessary' (and hence the accuracy of most of Marx's predictions, the scientific validity of his work) and 'better', conducive to the general good, a state of affairs that *ought* to exist.[25] The same may be said of the theory of the novel I am going to suggest: it is grounded at every point in the texts themselves, which are taken 'at their surface'; nothing needs to be read into them, what we discover is there for the most casual reader to see; but only if he wants to, only in so far as he is concerned that our culture should realize certain possibilities, certain values, about which we all are agreed[26] (provided, of

25 See Maurice Godelier's excellent *Rationalité et Irrationalité en Economie*, François Maspéro, 1966, pages 80–84 in particular.

26 This is one of the reasons why I began by mentioning the widespread disaffection among students. The young are (or should be, since the future is theirs) those for whom possibility is more real than actuality. An article entitled 'The Job of the Humanist Scholar', by a professor of history, concludes with this paragraph: 'The job of the humanist scholar is to organize our huge inheritance of culture, to make the past available to the present, to make the whole of civilization available to men, who necessarily live in one small corner for a little stretch of time, and finally, to judge, as a critic, the actions of the present by the experience of the past' (American Council of Learned Societies Newsletter, Vol. XII, December 1961, No. 10). Notice that the humanist scholar has nothing whatever to do with the future, and even in regard to the present his role is merely that of a 'critic'. The *real* social function of men like the author of this article (and he undoubtedly writes as would an overwhelming majority of university teachers) is to reconcile the student to the killing of his future. So that we are not asphyxiated in our 'small corner' and 'little stretch of time" an opening is made toward the rear, never ahead. "Our huge inheritance of culture" is like money in the bank, where time is the accumulation of interest. As Nietzsche remarks, the motto of the historian is: 'Let the dead bury the living '. The fallacy of the objective vantage

course, as always, we are informed and have not been so thoroughly absorbed into the system as to have become incapable of acknowledging its crimes and stupidities). The theory will be indistinguishably 'subjective' and 'objective', and necessarily so; or, as Godelier puts it: 'Scientific thought contests appearances and at the same time accounts for them'.[27]

Very little sense is to be made of any aspect of western life since the French Revolution if this contradiction between 'collective' labour and individual ownership is not borne continually in mind. The common good is radically incompatible with the pursuit of private welfare as the bourgeoisie understands it, and I believe this dilemma to be at the source of one of the most extraordinary characteristics of our culture: the fact that, from the beginning of the last century to the present, the greatness of a thinker, writer, or artist has been directly proportional to the ferocity of his opposition to what is, after all, his *own society*! The importance of any cultural product has depended upon the degree of outrage or incomprehension with which it is greeted; so that at one extreme we have men like Marx and Stendhal who achieve both scandal and 'unintelligibility' while, at the other, the various apologetic philosophies and mass entertainment are beneath contempt precisely *because* they express most perfectly the bourgeois view of things.

To distance oneself from this view it is sufficient to lapse into the 'prereflexive',[28] to talk openly about what is common knowledge but what, for that very reason, has to be ignored

---

point is what makes thinking like that of the historian I have quoted from possible: he does not see that one does not make 'the past available to the present'. What is made available is our 'subjective' view of the past, which ceases to be subjective in proportion as it is influenced by studied, tenacious and yet, within limits, flexible projects for a better future.

27 *Rationalité et Irrationalité en Economie*, François Maspéro, 1966, p. 143. Inseparably the facts call for the theory, and yet are not clearly 'visible' without it. A theory of the novel will have to precede our reading of the texts, and yet it emerges from that reading. There must be a constant 'shuttling' between theory (the 'questions' which are put) and fact; a constant 'adjustment' of one to the other.

28 'We can imagine a society in which reflexion would build up into a world of lies. We can all the more easily imagine such a society because it is our own' (Sartre, *Conscience de Soi et Connaissance de Soi*, Bulletin de la Société Française de Philosophie, 42ᵉ année, No. 3, Avril–Juin 1948, p. 82).

or slighted. Our attitudes toward sex are the simplest instance of this: to be naively urgent and direct is to stoop to the 'commonest' in our common humanity, it is to be 'obscene'. Most nineteenth-century 'culture' can be safely described as a vast 'reflexive' attempt to deny what, thanks to the Enlightenment, now goes without saying. From *la vie de bohème* to the present-day hippies and turbulent students there have existed marginal groups which, simply by not conforming, achieve something positive; they achieve one form of that 'distance without separation' which consists in trying to *live* the freedom and equality which the rest of society merely talks about. These groups do not represent different 'opinions', they proclaim the obvious (the brutal, hypocritical stupidity of everything that finds favour with the authorities and the well-to-do) otherwise they would not incur the fascination, envy or hatred of those too heavily committed to their society as it exists to desire a perspective upon it.

If this conflict between the good of the many (the realm of praxis, of the self-evident) and the interests of a few (consolidated by reflexion upon, or investigation of, a given) is as crucial to our culture as has been suggested, and if the novel is the supreme art form of that culture, then in the novel we should find the fullest expression of a contradiction the effects of which became conspicuous during the lifetime of the first great post-revolutionary novelist—Balzac.

We will find that the novel divides itself into two distinct levels of discourse which I shall call the explicit and the implicit. The explicit is the tribute the novelist pays the obvious; it is his denunciation of a society which, with a monstrous abuse of confidence, always places money before people. The novelist may convey his judgments and criticisms directly by suspending the narration momentarily as do Balzac and Dickens; or, in the more refined technique of a Zola or a Tolstoy, opposition will be incorporated into what is shown and how it is shown. On the implicit level the novelist gives expression to presuppositions which are those of his class and historical period, and these assumptions are of a nature to annul in one way or another the novelist's criticism of his society.[29]

29 Needless to say we shall be returning to all these points in greater detail later on. To avoid confusion, however, let me note at once: 1.

Such is the extraordinary predicament of the classical novelist: he cannot ignore the obvious—the greatest achievement of his *own class*—the ideal of a common humanity which follows from the notion that value and legitimacy come from labour; and yet at the same time to be a *great* novelist he must excel in his manner of dealing with the implicit level where he will be found to be putting forth conceptions which abolish any hope that something practical might be done about the abuses denounced on a different level of discourse. This 'necessity' of combating and supporting, denying and accepting all at the same time is one of the major reasons for the bizarre mixture of sense and sheer nonsense one finds in men like Balzac, Dickens and Tolstoy.

There is no greatness in the classical novel apart from the manner in which the implicit is dealt with; whereas the reverse is of course not the case: over-emphasis of the explicit leads to a thesis novel like Balzac's *Médecin de Campagne*. A novel the 'message' of which is exclusively implicit may be intolerably dull (it usually is) but it remains undoubtedly a novel; whereas if the explicit usurps *all* the place we have not a novel, but a political pamphlet, a work of philosophy or what you will. A theory of the classical novel, consequently, will be a theory concerning the precise nature of what is being said *implicitly* through this particular art form.

The explicit and implicit levels are not always as clearly discernible as they are in Balzac and Dickens; one level may easily shade into the other. Let us consider therefore that, by and large, the explicit is what the novelist 'says' consciously and deliberately (thus Flaubert's aestheticism—even though his contemporaries often missed it—belongs to the explicit, while his scientism would be implicit), the implicit being what is said much less consciously because the novelist imagines, with greater or lesser honesty, that he is simply 'copying reality'.

Stendhal will in each instance be an exception (we shall see, for example, that there is no implicit level in his novels); 2. If the novel is a form of praxis, then it is natural we be concerned only with that fiction which 'performs its task' most successfully. Our definition of the novel in other words will constitute at the same time a norm; so the fact that the vast majority of nineteenth-century novels have little or no explicit level indicates not a defect in my theory but, on the contrary, gives us one of the reasons for the mediocrity of most of these novels.

We have to determine what 'reality' the classical novel was trying to capture; a reality which must exist, and yet be one which was brought into existence (like all reality) and sustained there by a specific cultural intentionality; it must *mean something* in terms of the praxis of the nineteenth-century bourgeoisie.

The contradiction which Marx denounced between 'socialized' labour and private ownership of the means of production led us to a kind of 'homology' in the novel in the form of two levels of discourse: the explicit, acknowledging our common humanity and therefore condemning man's inhumanity to man; and the implicit, which is the voice of the novelist as a member of the very social class profiting most from the blocking of what might conceivably have been a *communal* exploitation of modern technology. Since the basic structure of our society is economic, we must see once again whether we cannot find in Marx some indication of what the classical novelist is 'showing' us as a function of his inherence in a particular social class.

From the Middle Ages to the present, the bourgeoisie ascended to power at exactly the rate at which the use value of commodities was supplanted by their exchange value. The contradiction in capitalism we have just been discussing could not have come about had not a new commodity appeared on the market in sufficient quantity—human labour; but even though, this time, *men* are involved, there is still the supplanting of use by exchange value; as though men, as in Adam Smith, were indistinguishable from 'labouring cattle'.

For Locke, Smith, Ricardo and others, as well as for Marx, value comes from labour; so that, in a barter economy, those articles are exchangeable which have accumulated the same amount of labour. According to the orthodox economist, this is what happens when the worker offers his labour on the market. With his salary he will be able to purchase goods having accumulated exactly the same amount of labour as he had himself sold to his employer. Capitalism is therefore based upon a fair exchange, the only difficulty being that it is now impossible to explain the source of profit.

Marx, however, was able to explain it by pointing out that if labour is to be regarded as a commodity, then to be consistent we must attribute to it, as to all commodities, a use as well as an exchange value. The capitalist pays for the *exchange* value of labour, he gives the amount of money necessary to ensure the purely physiological functioning of the worker (this is what men supply when they work to rule); he does not pay for the intelligent activity which is the use value of labour, which creates not only the value necessary to the physical survival of the worker, but a surplus value which is the capitalist's profit.[30]

We are dealing with two totally incompatible conceptions of man. For Marx, man *is* that intentionally orientated activity (resulting in a *useful* article) which he called labour power; so that the capitalist's purchase of labour is in reality the purchase of men. (We see this readily enough in the case of the artist or thinker who, in putting his creative 'power' at someone else's disposal, destroys himself; we hesitate to see it in the case of the man working on an assembly line.) It is only in a slave society, however, that men are bought; so that the bourgeois theorist was caught in the following dilemma: he had to consider that everything the worker gave was paid for *in full* by his employer, that a man can be a saleable object;[31] and yet if this is not to be slavery, we are obliged to think in terms of an object which is 'free'—free to sell or to refuse to sell itself. This monstrosity—a free *object*—is the subject matter of the classical novel.

The classical novel is about the identity of human beings, and this identity is at once 'free' (for it has to be 'proven') and yet it is an entity (for it is always given). We shall say that *identity is a given-proven.*

The bourgeois economist is unable to offer a serious explanation of the source of profit. The answer is to be found in the implicit content of the classical novel, and it is implicit because it is preposterous: profit—that is, wealth—is the

---

30 The 'labour' of the capitalist is devoted to the *distribution*, not the *creation* of surplus value.

31 When bourgeois philosophers and economists used the word 'man', they never meant labourers, servants, beggars, etc., but only that small minority of men possessing a certain minimum of property. Thus Smith sees no necessity to distinguish between labouring cattle and labouring men; while for Locke, his servant's labour and his own were one and the same thing. See the chapter on Locke in C. B. Macpherson's book *The Political Theory of Possessive Individualism*, Oxford, 1962.

confirmation of a good identity, the sign of an election; and conversely, when the workers starve this is equally sure an indication that they deserve to, they are the wrong kind of people. Hence, as Malraux remarked, the bourgeois rules by divine right; but it is a right which, unlike that of the noble, has to be demonstrated ('proven') through property, and snobbery is the loud denial that any doubt can exist as to the conclusiveness of the display.

The better nineteenth-century novelists do not, of course, make as bare-faced a use of identity as I suggest in the preceding paragraph (Dickens does, however; and, on occasion, Balzac), but before embarking upon an investigation of the novel itself it is indispensable to be as clear as possible about what is meant by 'identity'.

The difficulty is that in studying such a concept we study ourselves, and we are right to mistrust a man's own opinion of himself. If that opinion often strikes us as absurd, it is because the individual concerned has reflexively created a self (his 'identity', precisely), manufactured a given which he regards as 'causing' what he does. The advantage of ignoring the initiative which has been taken (that of regarding the self as entity rather than as praxis) is immense, for it enables us to define our self as constantly and essentially well-intentioned; so that no matter what we actually do or allow to be done, our self-esteem need not be affected since, by definition, the intention was honourable.[32]

A man gains perspective upon himself not by introspection, not by scanning the 'inner world' rather as the positivist looks for the fixed or the independently coherent in the 'outer', but by trying to be clear about the practical appropriateness of what he is doing in relation to the situation in which he finds himself. But then we are led to envisage the possibility that the notion of self is not only superfluous, simply a product of western culture during a certain phase of its evolution, but, in its various forms—individualism, the private life, character and

32 The American politicians and military leaders who were most responsible for the war in Vietnam were, in terms of what they *did*, war criminals; but criminals who, thanks to the nature of their society, were able to convert themselves into sincere men-doing-the-best-they-knew-how-in-very-difficult-circumstances.

intelligence in so far as they are regarded as being 'received' through heredity or environment, etc.—perhaps the greatest single obstacle to thinking our way clear of the debris left by the collapse of western culture as it has existed since the Renaissance.[33] An obstacle not only because it is a notion so general as to be difficult to circumscribe (or, in other terms, too 'close' to be able to focus upon clearly) but because, in the form of 'individualism' it is one of our fondest ideals; and yet an ideal which, upon the slightest examination deteriorates into prejudice since we are certainly no more 'individualistic' to, for instance, the Chinese, than they are to us.[34]

Just as the individual in judging himself must give full weight to the observations of others as to what he had actually done (as opposed to what he might like to think of himself as having done thanks to his estimation of the sort of person he 'really is') so, in investigating a social phenomenon like the western notion of individual identity, we are obliged to accept the judgment of those (the workers in the last century, peoples of the underdeveloped parts of the world today) who suffer the consequences of the praxis of a society as a whole having been deflected to the advantage of a class within that society; of those who are able to tell us exactly what we are *doing* as opposed to what we say we are doing in the Declaration of the Rights of Man and similar documents.

---

33 In talking about identity, consequently, I have in mind two things: 1. A consciousness so general (the best single expression for which may be— thanks to its various associations in French use—*la vie intérieure*) that even in philosophy it will usually be thought *with* rather than *at*: just as our perception of space, even among the best educated, has remained practically untouched by over half a century of modern art and the work of philosophers like Heidegger and Merleau-Ponty. 2. And then, of course, the 'specific instance' of identity as the basic structure of the classical novel.

34 See the introductory chapter of Louis Dumont's *Homo Hierarchus*, Gallimard, 1966. Paul Bénichou's *Morales du Grand Siècle* (Gallimard, 1948) is in large part an instructive historical treatment of some aspects of what we mean by individualism.

2 Further preliminaries

THE history of the middle classes is that of the progress of displaced people living on the flanks of great fortresses and pandering, through commerce, to more or less artificial needs. The ur-bourgeois was a drifter and a parasite. He was alone, an 'individual'; and although the bourg eventually became his own with the city states of the Renaissance, what he had acquired was, in the main, a home and not adherence to a group whose collective existence could be absorbed into the long-frozen Aristotelian-Christian hierarchical system. The mediaeval merchant, having to make a place for himself where he was neither needed nor, perhaps, wanted, developed some admirable qualities—alertness of mind, irreverence, humour . . . . He was for several centuries, until the rise of the proletariat, the observing *tiers*. The slow decay of the economic independence of the manor marked the transformation of the merchant's goods from luxuries into necessities; but this could never alter the monstrous fact that, for the merchant, use value was of consequence *only* in so far as it affected exchange value. The bourgeois was to remain a 'spectator' within his own society since no matter how socially useful his activities might become, their true purpose was the realization of exchange value; that is, in the last analysis, the aggrandizement of the self. If we quite naturally associate hypocrisy with the middle classes, it is because their 'service to the community' can never be more than coincidental. The bourgeois works against his fellows not with them; and this is why, in the religion he evolved for himself—Protestantism—he is accountable only to God; he can be saved by faith alone.

The merchant-manufacturer formed a society in which man defines himself by reference neither to a 'natural entity' group (tribe, aristocracy, peasantry, etc.) nor to a group whose cohesion is 'in front of it', in its project (revolutionary peasantry or proletariat). In fact, our society is one which, in appearance at least, suppresses the group since it is made up of 'individuals' related to one another not directly through the sharing of a common purpose or a common 'place' in the cosmic scheme, but indirectly through moral obligation.

In primitive societies the various activities which make up the struggle against scarcity may be clearly seen to have a practical utility; or, where this is not so, their utility is that of rendering coherent a particular vision of the universe, which coherence in turn makes for a personality which is in itself a form of control over the environment. The early bourgeois, however, was not only parasitical, he was denounced as such by the Church. How could he occupy a lawful and dignified place in his society when his function consisted in supplanting use value by exchange value. He could not, of course, except by persuading people that what was patently absurd and vicious—the placing of money before men—actually had a function within an order not yet entirely revealed perhaps but whose existence, especially after Newton, could not be doubted. In other words he had to evolve a new culture, one in which for the first time in history the selfish pursuit of wealth could be regarded as morally justifiable. This notion, however, so outrages what is deepest in our humanity (the fact we are 'species animals' in Marx's words, or, as Sartre puts it, there exists an irrefragable 'reciprocity') that it could never fully establish itself, and had the success it did have only because of what, on the cultural level, is one of the most striking characteristics of western civilization: *the breaking down of religion into science and morality; into explanation on the one hand, value on the other.*

This process, which reaches its fullest development of horror and absurdity in Malthus, gave disquiet almost from the beginning. The hunt for an alternative goes back to Pascal and achieves success with the dialectical philosophy of Marx in which man does not haplessly or serenely (depending upon his income) contemplate a valueless given; on the contrary, he forms part of an evolving totality which creates him, but which he in turn creates, just as the 'absurd' and threatening world of today has been created by the contemplative abstentionism of the 'objective' intellectual and of positivism in general. (The purpose of the 'two cultures' debate is to help explain why the humanist, despite the best will in the world, exercises an influence for the good which is totally imperceptible.)

The French Revolution may be looked upon from two radically different points of view: as being primarily a 'natural' process by which one social class and its ideology supplants another (explanation), or as the act itself by which men alter the conditions under which they live (value). The former view tends to be stressed by men seeking the 'laws of history'; by men therefore unable to free themselves from that essentially bourgeois view of the world which needs an order within which it may be assumed that the work of self-aggrandizement plays a role vital to all. This is the sad history of European 'socialism'. If, on the contrary, we regard the Revolution not as an historical process working itself out more or less mechanically, but as 'men pursuing their goals' (Marx) or, more precisely, as a conspicuous example of the way in which men can dissolve a *pratico-inerte* of their own creation but one which had none the less enslaved them (Sartre), then we move in the company of the authentic revolutionary.

A reading of Daniel Guérin's *La Lutte des Classes sous la Première République* leaves one with the picture of a bourgeoisie (including the firebrands like Robespierre and Danton) engaged not in prosecuting a revolution at all, but in fighting foreign wars and in preventing a revolution in the second sense. The problem was to accept the results of the revolution while rejecting its means; to regard it not as the establishment of something new, but as the recognition at last by a sufficient number of enlightened individuals of the great rational Plan; so that the only 'act' in which men can profitably engage is that of cognition.

The nobleman was a tiny fragment of the cosmos. He and the state were one and the same thing. In his person the public and private were indistinguishably fused, and throughout the greater part of its long evolution the middle class remained mesmerized by this supremely enviable condition— the possession of an identity which did not have to be earned, which wealth and display did not constitute but simply manifested. The problem of the bourgeois was to preserve the happy possibility of an identity granted and not earned (since the true goal of commerce and industry cannot be avowed) whilst at the same time attacking the feudal system so as to find a place within it. What he had to do was to transform the private

34

realm (that of the selfish pursuit of wealth) into the public, while retaining the former which is the real basis of his social existence. Wealth became an aspect of the operation of 'natural law' (public realm), the rich became in themselves an 'explanation'—robots, not working but worked upon, and devoid of subjective craving which is the domain of value, of the 'irresponsible', and the 'irrational', of the artist, of women and children. There came into being that astonishing bifocal mentality for which bad faith is a way of life, that of the businessman whose one concern is to serve the nation and to whom wealth accrues quite by chance, or possibly as an 'incentive' to spur him on to still greater efforts for the general good. The depersonalization characteristic of our time is therefore built into the protestant-capitalist ethos; it follows from the separation of value and explanation, from the hypocritical suppression of subjectivity; that is, of the immediate, of the evident, of use value.

It was the argument of the eighteenth-century rationalists that the privileges of the aristocracy had been usurped at some remote period of history, and that to be founded in reason, they would have to be founded in merit. But also, as we just saw, the bourgeois seeks an identity which need not be merited (earned), and the solution here is to regard merit not as something one does (this possibility is always and necessarily closed to the bourgeois) but as a mental attitude, as the acknowledgement of the great scheme. For example, the early economists said that the only legitimate property was that which resulted from labour; labour however considered not as the 'humanization of nature and the naturalization of man' (Marx), the source of all value, and ultimately of all intelligibility, but labour as an affair of the *individual* not of the collectivity; as a kind of entity which, as such, can be bought from the worker and which in the capitalist constitutes one aspect of his harmonious adjustment to the rational order.

But the clearest merit of the bourgeois is, of course, his morality—the ideal device for earning what is already there. The more rigid the moral code, the more effective it is in helping to detect identity; for while all men are equal, there are those who do not enter into consideration: criminals, perverts, the insane, fallen women, primitives, the militant

35

poor . . . , anyone who threatens order as envisaged by a tiny few. The immense importance of morality as a rule of thumb for the determination of identity derives from the fact that the bourgeois, being accountable to God alone and/or being simply made use of by impersonal law, has no responsibility for the public realm; or, more exactly, he deals with it in terms of identity: all malfunctions of the social order are brought about by people who deliberately will them, by people who therefore are by nature evil. In ordinary times such people are kept in prison, in times of crisis it is the function of strong government to eliminate them: to fire on workers as in the last century, to exterminate the Jews in our own.

The bourgeois looks upon his own revolution with those mixed feelings so well exposed in *A Tale of Two Cities*. He is satisfied with the results, but appalled by the means; for if violence can be a constitutive activity his whole scientific and moral philosophy is undermined. For him, violence leads necessarily either to anarchy or to the temporary triumph of evil (Communism); it is always an aberration since the body politic ejects those individual and identifiable particles which wish it ill. In a world of 'achievement' through property— cultural or material—the only admissible violence is that hidden kind by which occidental society with averted eyes and heavy heart condemns, in its portion of the underdeveloped world, any movement towards agrarian revolution, towards a planned and determined attack upon starvation.

It will be recalled that the difficulty in thinking about identity lies in seeing the oddness of what we take for granted, that of 'drawing back' far enough to be able to see that what we imagine ourselves to be thinking about, we are in reality thinking with; our avenues of approach predetermine our point of arrival, and the broadest of these avenues is probably that of the two worlds—the 'inner' and 'outer'. To illustrate, let us look, at a remark which Keynes makes on the last pages of his pamphlet *The End of Laisser Faire*. He has been assuring his readers that he has not been suggesting any structural changes in the economy, that there is nothing in his reflection which is seriously incompatible with: '. . . the essential characteristic of capitalism, namely the dependence upon an intense appeal to the money making and money loving instincts of individuals as the main motive force of the economic machine'. (We might marvel, in passing, that any institution should freely claim an 'essential characteristic' of such a nature). 'Instincts' are part of the furnishings of that non-existent inner realm to which we 'instinctively' appeal to make the world intelligible. Interest is the word most commonly used in an economic context, enlightened self-interest being the 'subjective pole' of economic law. In any inventory of our inner items, however, reason will come close to the top of the list. Here is a passage from Mill's essay on Coleridge: 'By the union of the enlarged views and analytic powers of speculative men with the observation and contriving sagacity of men of practice, better institutions and better doctrines must be elaborated; and until this is done we cannot hope for much improvement in our present conditions.' (By 'men of practice', Mills means no more than, for example, an architect as opposed to a social philosopher who would be a 'speculative man'.) Better institutions and doctrines are 'elaborated'; they are the products of purely mental activities. It is from this attitude that our entire educational system derives—to alter conditions you alter minds. To convert reality by converting people, however, is so obviously utopian that there has always been room among us for 'realists'; those who hold that the inner world does not determine the outer, but is determined by it.

Rationality of this kind has become an enslavement of which we are all too often unaware; as when we think in terms of originality and self-expression in the artist or philosopher, as when we talk of 'will power' or of the unconscious as an entity. Gide vitiated part of his ethic by recommending we allow our 'authentic being' to rise to the surface; and we may still, despite ourselves, refer to 'human nature'. Even when we realize that love at first sight, in so far as it exists at all, is not the quasi-miraculous encounter of two people 'made for each other', it is not easy to think in terms other than the pre-adjustment of two inner worlds, to see that X had not been waiting for a woman with precisely these characteristics but rather that the woman revealed to him the precise nature of his needs and wishes. Similarly, the artist or writer does not 'elaborate' a pre-existing image or text; on the contrary, he discovers what he

37

meant in the finished work (which is consequently never really finished), just as the 'self' of Marx's worker is 'outside', in the products of his labour.

When I said that the novel is about identity, I meant that it was about aspects of this mythical inner realm. We tend to contrast science and myth whereas (apart from Marx's concept of thought as praxis) there is only myth. In appearance at least, science and myth are antithetical; for while myth constantly appeals to a 'beyond'[1] to explain the actual, bourgeois thought claims to be led more or less passively from the actual to whatever lies beyond, if anything. It is said that we think or investigate our way to the truth, while the primitive accepts a traditional explanation. But this is not quite the case.

When a tyre blows out, throws his truck off the road and wrecks it, the African driver knows as well as the westerner why it happened (the tyres had been recapped, the truck was over-loaded, etc.). But neither will stop there. For both, an event of this kind has a significance. The African will ask: 'Who is trying to kill me?', and will take whatever steps are necessary to disarm or placate his enemy. Apart from malevolence of this kind he is perfectly safe, and his driving may consequently be unbelievably reckless. The westerner will make remarks such as: 'This *would* happen to *me*'; or, conversely, 'Why should this happen to *me*?' The African thinks in terms of an eruption of the beyond into the actual; the westerner is concerned with the *kind of person he is*, and so imagines that his attitude is more 'practical', closer to 'reality'. In fact he is dealing with a given; with what is not, therefore, explicable in purely human terms and which must therefore involve an implicit reference to a beyond.

Since we create our world, both men are in a sense right. If the African has reason to suppose that juju is being used against him this may produce a frightened distraction which will bring about an accident. If the westerner had always been told he

---

1 This is a term which must be defined for I shall be making repeated use of it. Here it needs no elucidation, but when used in reference to the novel it should be taken to mean whatever the novelist regards as existing independently of human praxis while exercising an influence on men's lives; usually this will amount to scientism in one form or another (realism), or an 'other worldliness' which may be merely that of ordinary religion, but which can also be that of *Moby Dick*.

was untrustworthy and careless he would tend to be exactly that. The novel, however, will have none of this, for it is an art form in which mythical event is replaced by a mythical identity; a form, that is, in which the beyond need not interfere, it is already installed in the actual. It is by no means uncommon, however, in the nineteenth-century novel, for the beyond to erupt almost as blatantly as it does for the primitive. In addition to the abuse of providential coincidence, the storm which comes and goes to accompany the final coming together of Dorothea and Ladislaw in *Middlemarch,* and the identical dreams of Anna and Vronsky in *Anna Karenina,* indicate how fraught with significance life can be.

Nevertheless in pre-bourgeois myth interest is concentrated exclusively on what happens; the hero has no *personal* existence.[2] Oedipus committed his crimes in total ignorance, Achilles became almost invulnerable through no merit of his own, the love of Tristan and Isolde was the consequence of their having been given a philtre. The folk ballads simply recount, with no trace of commentary as to why these fearful things should have happened to A rather than to B. Someone is 'designated' (with or without benefit of an 'annunciation') to be a messenger of the gods, and that is as far as anyone looks. With renaissance tragedy, protestantism, and the theological science of the time, the world undergoes a simultaneous secularization and divinization: a secularization in the sense that the beyond is no longer free to fall arbitrarily athwart the course of daily life, divinization in the sense that the two distinct spheres (divine and sublunary, perfect and imperfect,

2 In his *Le Mythe de l'Eternel Retour* (Gallimard, 1961), Mircea Eliade writes as follows about primitive ontological conceptions: '. . . an object or an act becomes real in so far as it imitates or repeats an archetype. Thus, reality is acquired exclusively by repetition or participation; everything without an exemplary model is "meaningless", that is, lacks reality. Men would therefore tend to become archetypal and paradigmatic. This tendency may well seem paradoxical in the sense that the man of cultures based on tradition recognizes himself as real only in proportion as he ceases to be himself for a modern observer and is satisfied to imitate and to repeat the gestures of another. In other words he recognizes himself as being real, that is, as truly himself, only in so far as he ceases, precisely, to be himself' (p. 63). Eliade goes on to link this with platonism, and we can safely take it that a greater or lesser lack of personal identity prevailed up to the advent of modern rationalism.

necessary and contingent, etc.) of ancient and mediaeval thought tend to be fused into a universe which is a *finished product* rather than an approximation of something better; one in which, consequently, God is omnipresent and yet absent. (In the seventeenth century the English school maintained against the Cartesian that space was not matter, that it was part of the infinite which was God. Newton proved this view to be more rewarding scientifically, but it results in too much of a good thing; if God is everywhere he is nowhere, and we are not much better off than with the Cartesians who had been led to locate God way out there where matter ended and space began.)

In a world where the sacred took the form of event, men either bargained with the gods (priests or magicians could call down or avert a plague) or were their helpless victims (Greek tragedy, folk ballads). In the scientific world which was the creation of the Renaissance, men are neither so powerful nor so weak—they neither intercede nor accept, they seek to know, because event has become calculable. In the Middle Ages knowledge was gained by noting location in the hierarchy, and position—higher or lower—was automatically an evaluation (metals were literally 'base' or 'precious'). Perception was 'direct' in the sense that an object was known by reference to other objects.[3] Science suppressed the 'reference', so that perception became primarily a question of the relationship between a subject and an object rather than a question of relationships between objects. This amounts to saying that science is interested in things in isolation:[4] perception is a

3 It was also 'direct' in respect to what I have been calling the beyond, a term which is therefore a misnomer when applied to pre-rationalist cultures. For the primitive, a dead person can appear in a dream because the dead are present, they continue to be part of the community; whereas, among us, spirits must be summoned from a distance and, as is well known, the discomforts of a long journey sometimes make them refractory in answering questions. For mediaeval philosophy 'essences' were part of God, only 'accidents' were not, and God was therefore a part of the world. In other words, the beyond was shut up within the 'closed' universe of former cultures while with the coming of the scientific notion of infinity it became an invisible hand. In his *Proofs of the Existence of God* Aquinas says that there is movement because we can see it with our own eyes. For science, of course, nothing is less reliable than undisciplined sight.

4 In the pseudo-sciences, this was to develop into the fetishism of the fact. For Marx, the isolated fact is always abstract and can acquire meaning

process which, by setting aside secondary qualities, arrives at the 'essence' of things. By essence is meant what is measurable, or calculable; thus, for Descartes, the essence of matter is its 'extension'.

It must not be supposed that renaissance science came as a wonderful revelation of the truth; for it could justifiably appear to many minds of the time that too much was being sacrificed for what was gained. In order to know that, under certain conditions, a feather will fall with the same speed as a cannon-ball, the feather must cease to exist as such and become 'extended matter'. The visible world is sacrificed to an invisible one, declared to be alone real because universal, all the rest being mere appearance.

Scientific investigation is consequently paradoxical in that it involves an identification through isolation (the main function of a laboratory is to permit effective isolation) which will be justified when identity can be abolished by universalization (laws of nature applicable to all extended bodies can be worked out, etc.).

Coming to the sciences of classification which begin to make notable progress in the eighteenth century (and whose importance for the novel may be judged by reading Balzac's *Avant-Propos* to the *Comédie Humaine*), it is to be remarked that order is simply 'secularized hierarchy' (again that peculiar 'presence-absence' of the beyond which is one of the most striking

---

only by reference to the whole which is in its turn completed and verified by the fact. This 'shuttling' between the whole and the detail is one of the most conspicuous aspects of dialectical reasoning. Thus, in *Estranged Labour*: 'Just as we have found the concept of private property from the concept of the estranged, alienated labour by analysis, in the same way every category of political economy can be evolved with the help of these two factors; and we shall find again in each category, e.g. trade, competition, capital, money, only a definite and developed expression of the first foundation.' (*Philosophic and Economic Manuscripts of* 1844, Lawrence and Wishart, 1959, p. 82.) But where does the 'first foundation' come from? Ultimately from human purpose, from a praxis. 'If the product of labour does not belong to the worker, if it confronts him as an alien power this can only be because it belongs to some other man than the worker. If the worker's activity is a torment to him, to another it must be delight and his life's joy. Not God, not nature, but only man himself can be this alien power over man' (*ibid.*, p. 79). It is as a result of their refusal to relate fact to a context of purpose that the 'sciences of man' (including the study of the novel) have remained sterile.

characteristics of bourgeois culture). The king does not have his place in the hierarchy, the existence of hierarchy demands that this particular place be filled. There can be only one hierarchy (from the 'lowest' to the 'highest') but many orders are conceivable; and so while we could use the hierarchy to identify the individual, we must now identify the individual to establish an order; and once this is done, the 'individuality' disappears in a universalization. It is most important that we understand what is involved in the 'identification' of individuals.

One is immediately struck by the concreteness of mediaeval art, its almost photographic reality; and that it should be full of the grotesque and the sacred indicates simply that these things were as real for the artists of that time as landscapes are for us. Reality, though it changes far more slowly than social custom, is nevertheless also a convention. Rationalist universalism has taught us to believe in a single, given reality; change being due to a faulty or immature recording apparatus whether mind or hand. The truth is, however, that great art is a product of a struggle between the artist and his material, part of the resistance arising from the fact that the material is being formed to capture an *outer* reality which does not lend itself, at least for long, to such an operation because, as Husserl says, it is of the essence of objects that they entail an etcetera; that they be, in other words, 'inexhaustible'. And yet they are always organized into a more or less intelligible world; so the never-ending task of the artist becomes that of elucidating this (for classical rationalism) inconceivable 'juncture' of inner and outer which is the visible. 'It is peculiar to the visible,' writes Merleau-Ponty, 'that it should be in the strict sense lined with an invisible which it renders present in the form of a kind of absence'.[5] One could contrast this 'legitimate' art with that, much easier and more common, which copies a conventional reality, one which time has 'interiorized' so that what is being copied is, to a large extent, a mental image. The renaissance grotesque, most present-day African sculpture, any contemporary western art which has failed to break radically with the past, etc.—these are inferior arts because the artist

5 *l'Oeil et l'esprit*, Gallimard, 1964, p. 85.

no longer sees what he is copying, he is referring to a mental image, and the resistance of his material (that is, the difficulty of deciding what we really see) is reduced accordingly.

Mediaeval art, however, is not only concrete because it depicts the real, but even more important, because it is concerned with event. The difference between mediaeval and modern art lies in this: for the former, people were made saints by what happened to them; for the latter, what happened followed from their sainthood. We are so accustomed to thinking of events as 'following their course' that we have trouble imagining a culture for which event (because it is the direct intervention of the beyond) is constitutive of identity which is not given, but 'designated'. An art in which event is the central interest will of necessity be one full of concrete detail, it will be 'naïve'; for otherwise one could not make out what was happening. It is sufficient to compare a mediaeval to a renaissance martyrdom—in the one, the implements and procedure are carefully 'explained' to our view; the other is usually little more than a portrait of the martyr himself. This is the famous renaissance individualism; but what has not been sufficiently remarked is that this individualism is in reality an 'in-itselfness' utterly unthinkable apart from a preconceived, invisible order. Hegel and Marx should have led us to suspect (long before phenomenology and gestalt psychology brought confirmation) that perception, including the scientific, is a process narrowing from the whole to a part and not the reverse. Every perceived object stands out upon the vast background of a cultural orientation; and what makes rationalist perception peculiar is that it posits the non-existence of this 'situation' which is another way of saying that it posits the infinite. In western art the infinite is known as perspective—an interesting example of the substitution of order for hierarchy. In such art persons and objects are arranged not in respect to one another, but in respect to the infinite; each can be isolated from the other because there exists a non-perceptual but universal principle of organization. Mediaeval art, in contrast, presents as much of the whole field of vision as is practicable, and/or the important figures (Christ, the Virgin, a saint) are shown larger than the others. This technique is closer to perception as we are coming to understand it. Perspective is a highly artificial arrangement of only some features of what Husserl calls the *Lebenswelt*. Like most manifestations of rationalist culture, it sets out to eliminate the 'superficial' and the transitory in order to reach an 'underlying' truth; in fact, like science, it begins by suppressing or distorting what it proposed to understand—the existence of other people, for example. I am about to be introduced to a great man whom I have long admired and sought to meet. Entering a room where he is standing with a number of other people it is *he* I see, the room and the people in it fall into the background; and he, though twenty yards away is, as far as perception is concerned, actually closer than the chair I have my hand upon. Perspective gives a very different and erroneous account of this event. Or again, the figures in landscapes, the nudes and the models of classical art, are not human beings at all, but objects. A fellow-being is first of all a visual *experience*, not a visual *thing*. There is a passage in *Being and Nothingness* where Sartre describes what happens when another person suddenly comes into our field of vision. It ceases to be *our* field; there are now two centres (or, as Valéry says: 'a person alone is instantly and unconsciously modified by the arrival of another') and the orthodox artist can maintain his own perspective only at the cost of refusing to acknowledge the existence of this second consciousness; at the cost, in other words, of relating the other to infinity rather than to himself (the artist).[6]

The painter begins by dissociating himself from the scene or person he has chosen to record (if a novelist he becomes James's 'watcher at the window') on the supposition that thanks to this precaution the thing-in-itself unobscured by subjective interference will be revealed. What happens, however, as we have seen, is that the artist, by placing himself 'at a distance' creates (who ever voluntarily sits still for hours *except* to have his portrait painted?) the identity he set out to portray. Not being a *participant* in the reality which interests

6 Much more, of course, could be said along these lines. Classical art, for instance, captures an instant of time. The instant, however, does not exist; or rather it is composed of what Husserl calls 'retentions' and 'protentions' : the past and future, in other words, is an integral part of it. This, I think, provides justification on the perceptual level for the jumble of disparate objects often found in mediaeval art in contrast to which the art of the Renaissance will be, in Leonardo's phrase, a *cosa mentale*.

him, he is obliged to introduce from elsewhere some principle of intelligibility. If things and people are to be taken in isolation one from the other, then they must be supposed to possess a 'built-in', 'self-contained' identity; they are accessible to us because we have knowledge of them. *To identify we must cease to participate and instead bring knowledge to bear.*

This knowledge can safely be of an exceedingly rudimentary kind. At one point in the court proceedings related in Camus's novel *l'Étranger*, the girl friend of the hero is referred to as his 'mistress', and instantly the court audience has the opportunity to dissociate itself from her; thanks to its knowledge of sexual morality the girl is transformed from a perfectly intelligible activity into a judged object, she becomes a particular kind of girl.

It is not *experience* of Jews, Negroes, Communists, etc., which identifies them; one 'knows' what a Jew, Negro, Communist *is*, and one is therefore able to identify him. It will be objected that this is prejudice, not knowledge. But if, as I have been arguing from the beginning, our relationship with others and the world around us (despite what our science-dyed culture would have us suppose) is not a cognitive one, then prejudice appears in its true light as the aping of knowledge and not as the flouting of it. (The racist, like the researcher in a narrow field, will usually lay claim to a special competence: 'I know these people; lived among them all my life . . .' etc.). It appears as a permanent 'opportunity' of our particular cultural structure and not as an unfortunate aberration due, largely, to ignorance. The 'victim of racial prejudice' (as we sometimes stupidly put it, referring to the racist himself) is never at a loss for arguments; indeed he will eagerly develop them and clearly feels obliged to do so, thus betraying himself as part of a culture for which direct concrete experience needs to be rendered assimilable by knowledge; and in the process the experience can, if one sees fit, be twisted out of all recognition.[7]

7 One of the difficulties in pursuing a structural study is to avoid moving out in all directions at once in order to show that if this or that point can be legitimately made it is because, had we been working in another 'sector', it would (suitably adapted) have remained valid. Thus, in the present instance, the convenience of having recourse to knowledge to process experience (of not being obliged to use one's eyes and ears, in other words) is an extension to human relations of the mistrust of the senses which is an

It might be supposed that one must 'know to identify' in any culture. But in the case of the schoolmen, of priestly castes, knowledge is the attribute of a particular place in the hierarchy, and when this becomes secularized into the invisible rationalist order, knowledge becomes indispensable to one's very humanity (man is a 'thinking animal'). Bourgeois reality is an everyday reality; so that the ignorant (the masses), lacking the knowledge necessary to deal with it, fall outside humanity; whereas in most other cultures there would be a reality corresponding to this humble level, special competency being required only when this reality is temporarily suspended by visits from other realms. In our culture nothing is given to the individual, but everything can be attained (in contrast to hierarchical and primitive societies where the reverse obtains) and this is what gives western civilization its dynamism. It also gives it some less attractive qualities, for how is attainment to be recognized? Formerly, as we have seen, there was no attainment; or rather, the event arbitrarily designated it, apart from any consideration of personal merit in our sense. The transformation of event into identity gives rise to a contradiction which will be central to the novel—why should it be necessary to prove identity? Why should we have to attain to what is? How is it even possible?

The early protestants believed man to have been predestined to hell or salvation from the beginning of time, he was of the elect or of the damned, he had an 'identity'. But there we come upon one of the great difficulties in which western thought involved itself in exchange for scientific achievement—this identity, astonishingly, *cannot be subjectively apprehended*, it can only be inferred with the help of some outer reality. Given these effects, then this kind of thing must have caused them—since I am clean, industrious, and frugal, I must be one of the

---

indispensable aspect of the scientific method. To react you must first know; but since the pursuit of knowledge is unending the pursuit has become a profession, a vested interest like any other. Hence the tireless and unvarying prattle of the humanists, the liberals, the socialists—the men of good *will*— can never come to anything. These people embody the 'mental' in its attempts to deal effectively with the 'physical'; and thanks to this separation they can fail to see that their spectatorship is a praxis the effect of which is to perpetuate western impotence to bring about structural changes. To know is to be able to accept.

elect; or, in philosophy, given synthetic *a priori* knowledge, what must be the nature of mind that this should be possible? The classical rationalist approaches his own mind by way of the other; he contemplates his very self as an object in the world. The great mind-body dichotomy, in other words, never really existed; there was only 'body' in two different forms. In idealism, mind *is* the exterior world (but then why is not the latter at once exhaustively known?) and in empiricism the exterior world is duplicated as mental image (but then how are the two distinguished?). In each case we are left with the feeling that there must be 'something else',[8] but for as long as that something is conceived as another 'thing' we have a sequence of mirrored things receding into infinity.

In practice, however, as was just remarked, the other intervenes; not as a solipsistic, enregistering ego but as a 'constituting' subject whose power we indirectly acknowledge when we adopt its point of view upon ourselves. We create for ourselves an identity (dictated by others) which it then becomes the work of our lives to be taken in by. We cannot hope to convince others if we are not ourselves convinced, and this is accomplished by reflection (what sort of person do I want to be, what do I owe myself, can I be seen doing this, what is it appropriate for me to say at this time, etc., etc.)[9] as opposed to subjective evidence concerned with questions of *doing* divorced from reference to the two imaginary entities, self-principle. The joyless lives of many of the early capitalist entrepreneurs was intended to demonstrate that no goal of personal satisfaction had been set, they had simply been called upon to perform certain tasks in this world, they had been chosen; they could therefore contemplate themselves as another. The intro-

---

8 This something else came to be called 'intentionality'. The mental is not thing, but that act which constitutes things, or makes them 'representationable'.

9 Benjamin Franklin's plan for arriving at perfection which he communicates in his autobiography, is a striking instance of the creation of a reflexive self which we can 'stand off' from. But what is this 'we'; are there two selves? (and therefore an infinite number?). No, there is only this virtuous created object, and then the creating *activity* the purpose of which Franklin states repeatedly with an openness which today we find very surprising: 'Nothing so likely to make a man's fortune as virtue' (*Everyman*, 1960, p. 81).

duction of the motive of self-interest by the utilitarians changed nothing since the place of the Lord was taken by economic law of which self-interest became the implement. The capitalist remains an impelled object; and while he may take pride in being a self-made man, we are expected to understand that he always had it in him to succeed; success is acknowledgment from on high that he was made of the right stuff.

The uninterrupted necessity of maintaining the point of view of the other upon ourselves sets up a greater or lesser strain depending upon the degree of phoniness of which we are capable. Fitzgerald's *The Crack-up* is a fascinating account of how he, for one, came to find the effort too great. Wealth (which is to say power) will enable us to force the kind of recognition we want. But wealth remains extraneous, it is often of questionable origin, it can be lost, and with it our identity; so that what is needed is a wealth we can pass off as an integral part of our being. This wealth we call culture. Culture is as close as the bourgeois has ever been able to come to a restoration of the innate identity of the aristocrat, an identity independent of the consent of others because divinely ordained. The aristocrat had no need of the other (at least so it seemed to him) and culture sets the same goal of self-sufficiency. There are two differences, however: first, as part of its struggle against hierarchical society, the bourgeoisie demanded that culture be accessible to all (that is, that everyone be free to demonstrate an identity) but, secondly, bourgeois equality is that of monads, of isolated entities, and self-sufficiency under these conditions is a laborious attainment; it involves nothing less than an attempt to possess the entire past as a substitute for the present and future: as a substitute, that is, for valid human relationships which can exist only on the basis of a collective project, of a 'we'.

The foregoing discussion could have been organized around Marx's wonderfully illuminating distinction between the public and private realms.

We know that tragedy is not possible unless the audience is made to feel the presence of the extra-terrestrial. But we have seen that the beyond is by no means foreign to the classical novel. The real difference, therefore, between renaissance tragedy and the novel lies in the disappearance, after Racine, of a type of humanity (the noble) in which the public and private realms could not be separated. The Renaissance tragedy marks that brief period in the evolution of western culture during which the hierarchical public individual of mediaeval culture comes into irreconcilable conflict with the bourgeois private individual. The tragic hero is both these persons, and the conflict between the two within himself is what destroys him. It is very difficult for us today to enter into the spirit of renaissance *gloire;* we tend to see in it a peculiarly 'aristocratic' form of morality or of honour, whereas it has to do with the fact that the tragic hero is *in himself* the public realm. We distinguish between private individuals and public institutions, the latter prospering or declining in accord with historical and economic law; but where the 'institution' is a human being, the law (the beyond) can make its presence immediately felt in the persecution of the tragic hero. But with the separation of the public realm from individuals (with the end of hierarchical culture, in other words; or, as Marx put it, with the division of each of us into the citizen on the one hand and the private individual on the other) the beyond can exist only as a given (the order of rationalism and morality with its necessary correlate, identity) and when it is allowed to make too overt an appearance (abuse of coincidence, etc.) we feel the novelist is guilty of conduct unworthy of an honest realist. If we compare a 'bourgeois tragedy' like Musset's *Lorenzaccio* with a play by Shakespeare or Racine, we observe at once that the 'tragedy' of Lorenzaccio resides in his having become unsure, in carrying out his plan to rid Florence of a tyrant, as to the nature of his identity. In bourgeois art, as we shall see, the real issue is *never* the public realm which, when it is dealt with at all, serves merely to provide circumstances in which an identity can emerge from hiding or, on the contrary, confirm itself as stated. There is nothing of the kind in genuine tragedy which is tragic precisely because the issue far transcends that of the worth of a private individual. Bourgeois art narrates what the hero did or failed to do so that we may form a judgment; true tragedy, however, is not a narration, it is a situation from which there is no escape. If we attempt to judge Macbeth or Phaedra we have missed the point, because these are not private dramas.

There are many levels of unawareness, ascending from our total ignorance of such things as the phonemic structure of the sounds we utter in speech, to our almost full consciousness that on this or that occasion, losing our temper or falling in love served our purposes admirably. In the case of identity, the extent to which a novelist is aware of the contradictions and special pleading involved will depend upon how completely he is wed to middle-class values: they are foreign to Stendhal, inseparable from Dickens; so that, as we shall see, identity is an obstacle to the understanding of Stendhal (hence the unique position he occupies in nineteenth-century fiction) but indispensable to an analysis of Dickens's novels.

The unawareness a man develops as a consequence of belonging to a class obliged to talk equality whilst practising a discrimination as painstaking as any in history is one which, in some circumstances, he may overcome. He is part, however, not only of a class, but of a culture to which he owes the very manner in which he uses his eyes and ears, the very fact he considers that there exists an 'exterior world' for him to see and hear.

Consider the manner in which a town would be described in a classical novel; and, for that matter, in most present-day novels. The novelist might well start with such general considerations as climate, geographical location and so on, gradually narrowing down to the town itself and then perhaps, finally, to the house inhabited by the family about which the story has been written. Now there is no real vantage point from which such a picture could have been offered to the reader. Even if we imagine the novelist describing what he sees from a balloon, what we would then have is the town of X *seen from a balloon* and not the town lived in by the characters of the novel. It is the purpose of the novelist to present the 'real' town; but there is no such place except for the non-existent eye of God. The novelist writes about what he only 'knows', what he assumes must be there. The same analysis holds good for a relationship between two fictional characters. We admit at once that the novelist could never in real life know all that he puts down, but then we justify this liberty by supposing the truth to exist somewhere, and so the novelist has a right to suggest what in all probability it is. But once again, there is no such truth except from a non-human point

50

of view. Apart from this impossible objectivity there is only a group of strictly subjective appreciations of the relationship.

The error the nineteenth-century novelist commits in regard to place, he repeats in his concept of time. Just as a bird's-eye view of a town is just that, and not the town itself (which has no existence apart from the individual 'intention' which, taken with many others of similar nature, 'constitutes' it), so the past is never accessible in itself, but only *through* the present. Michel Butor's novel *l'Emploi du Temps* is a very interesting attempt to deal with this problem. He discovers that the search for past time is vain since during the quest one continues to live, and there can therefore be no fixed perspective. It is like trying to paint a landscape from a moving train. The past is an aspect of the present. It is not a given, any more than is the town we have been using to illustrate the fallacy inherent in the classical notion of space. We say that many billions of years elapsed before man appeared on earth. But this could not have been lived time; nor, on the other hand, could it have been scientific time since this time also is the creation of a specific human project—that of overcoming the non-measurability of lived time.

For classical rationalism time is a sort of medium, an 'invisible space' which 'goes by' as a projectile (the earth) moves with perfect regularity from one point to another; and the plot, in fiction, is a segment of this dead time. It is time transformed into an object with a beginning and an end, a thing *detached from us* which we can 'turn over in our hands' and examine from every point of view. It is in this way that the novelist endows the everyday, the average (the 'real') with an entirely adventitious interest. We would not ordinarily give the slightest attention to a taxi stopping at a door to drop its passenger, but we watch carefully this identical incident when it stands at the beginning of a film or novel because we know something is going to happen; in other words, an anticipated dénouement is present in every scene, transforming the commonplace into the significant or the extraordinary. We hold both ends of an independent unit of time within which we move freely back and forth. A definite beginning and end provide a framework making possible a composition of events which reality itself can never offer. This is what

Sartre means when, in *La Nausée*, he remarks that, in real life, 'there are no adventures'. The adventure is another of the many ways in which the novelist unconsciously chooses his reality. French neo-realism (because it abolishes the self and therefore the objective point of view the 'I' imagines itself capable of occupying) is simply the first uncompromising attempt not to interfere with the real. Complete success is of course out of the question, but we can get much closer than the use of the first person, a stream of consciousness and so forth; we can, for example (among other things), do away with the adventure, with the result that though much may happen, we do not know exactly what it is. In life as it is lived, we do not know and can never know why the couple next door are always quarrelling; and in telling us why, the orthodox novelist forgets he can do so only by terminating time; that is, by providing or suggesting an impossible explanation of what went before. The new realist novel does not end in this sense, it is not 'terminable'; so that what went before can at any moment be brought into question, and this is as it should be since (however rarely this may happen) we are free to change by a single act the significance of our entire life up to that point. Gide was therefore a precursor when he tried to give the reader the impression that his *Les Faux-Monnayeurs* could have gone on indefinitely, thus drawing closer to the 'inexhaustibility' of real life. In contrast to this there is the chapter-postscript of many nineteenth-century novels in which all the loose ends are taken up, in which (since what happens is of no interest in itself but only as an indication of identity) the various identities established in the course of the narrative are confirmed: X, as we expected, proved to be an excellent husband, whereas Y, needless to say, continued to drink and ended in the debtors' prison.

I began by attributing to the classical novelist a higher degree of awareness of identity than of those conceptions he owes less to class than to his inherence in a culture whose vision grows out of the requirements and achievements of science. But we can see now how artificial any such separation is bound to be. For if, as we shall see, the fictional character is engaged in a struggle to be what he already is (since identity is a given-proven), then he cannot do without the 'timeless time' we have been talking about. He needs a time which is not 'an integral part of the categories', but something he can 'pass through' essentially unchanged. Time is what is required for the confirmation of an announced identity, or the emerging of a hidden one; it is what 'goes by' during the opening of the package so we can all see what was inside; it is the presenting of obstacles which the hero will surmount or which will defeat him depending upon the temper of the self with which he sets out. In other words the classical novelist is engaged in an undertaking similar to that of the analyst practising a naïve form of Freudism—that which consists in disinterring the traumatic event supposed to cause the patient to act as he does—except that, most novel characters being normal, there is no single event lost in an unconscious, but instead a particular milieu, education, etc., the detailed reconstruction of which is a good part of the realism of the nineteenth-century novel. In fact, however, the neurotic must be regarded as a person whose existential project led him *to attribute* a crucial importance to the event in question in those instances where it was not simply invented. If we adopt this view, then the past, as we have seen, is an aspect of the present; like everything else it receives its significance and almost its existence from some cultural and individual initiative, and time is this initiative seeking to attain its goals.

In so far as men rely upon causality to explain phenomena they suppress time; for if an event is to be satisfactorily accounted for in this way, then it has to pre-exist in the cause, and this is precisely the situation obtaining in the classical novel where identity is always a given-proven. Time is creative human initiative; it is *change* or it is nothing, simply the 'linear space' in which a cause or identity unfolds itself.

That will suffice to give the reader a general idea of the private realm, of the 'inner world' which is the domain of the novel. I should like now to look into the novel as 'anti-praxis', the novel as *pratico-inerte*. In other words, what are the formal exigencies of classical fiction? A cultural praxis creates a world in which what is 'intentional' acquires a kind of 'necessity'. Identity, therefore, must be seen to be not only an aspect of the praxis of a social class, but also the 'answer' to the formal problems confronting the novel when Balzac began to write.

3 The classical novel as an art form

WHAT we know about, for example, scholasticism, we know thanks to that great 'negation' of it which is scientific rationalism. Scholasticism is, for us, precisely in so far as it is not part of our world view. But it is in the nature of that view to posit two entirely disparate entities—mind and matter—related in exteriority by knowledge, so that (for the rationalist) it is not the vantage point of a new praxis which makes scholasticism 'visible' to us, but the arrival at an absolute vantage point from which scholasticism is seen in itself, incomplete here and there because information is lacking, but unaffected in every other respect. The scholar contemplates, discovers or interrogates from an 'objective' eminence where the condition of vision is that it embrace *only* the completely detached, the 'other'. In the world of the given, in which necessarily the highest attainment for man is to know, to learn, the goal of the scholar becomes the discovery of other things, of things behind things since, where we prefer to ignore that the universe receives its signification as a function of our orientation within it, there is nothing else to be done. We have learned never to ask the question 'Why?'; but because there is no explanation apart from this question, the whole of scientific rationalism as a metaphysics has collapsed into the absurd.

With the novel as with everything else the scholar's only explanation will be to dig up ever more information from behind our present information, and with these new facts it should be possible to gauge the position of this particular novel in relation to that ideal, quintessential, hidden novel, the 'accidents' of which from antiquity to the present have been recorded in historico-critical panoramas. There is a less heavily-trudging school for which the text itself is the thing: fiction is primarily a craft, so a study of the various recipes would be the most rewarding approach. But here even more the question is how, rather than why the novel. The usual Marxist treatment would provide us with a fuller and more satisfactory causality, but cultural phenomena are not caused in the positivist sense; and if such an account were to dwell upon the novel as an instrument of bourgeois domination (as part of a praxis), then it would enter into hopeless contradiction with its basic assumption of the novel as an aspect of a superstructure determined by the means of production.

There can be no solution if we try to achieve the perspective we need by setting up an observed over and against an observer, for except in so far as the observed can be shown to have been— at whatever level—'intended', it is meaningless.

Our first step is an obvious one: the novel is the art form of the European middle classes. If, however, we regard *Don Quixote* as the first great novel, will it be practicable to seek a theory which would hold over so long a period? This attempt has been made, and we shall have to take it into account before going further.

George Lukacs and Lucien Goldmann[1] define the novel by contrasting it with epic literature and the tragic theatre. The career of the fictional hero does not confirm the known; it does not run its course in a world of generally accepted values; on the contrary, its whole significance lies in the fact that it is an always unsuccessful search for value. Value exists, of course, but implicitly, since it is only the hero who questions—without his questions ever receiving any very firm answers. One could in the light of this theory regard the novel as fundamentally 'existential' in the sense that it reveals the inadequacy of accepted wisdom and enduring principle when the weight of daily life is placed upon them.

If we were to stop at that (which is Lukacs's portion of the theory) we should have said nothing as to the reason for regarding the novel as inseparably associated with the rise of the bourgeoisie. Goldmann's contribution consists in pointing out that there exists what he calls a 'rigorous homology'[2] between the world of the novel as described by Lukacs, and what is perhaps the most important single characteristic of our society: the substitution of exchange value for use value which has proceeded almost without interruption since the middle ages.

1 See George Lukacs's *La Théorie du Roman*, Gonthier, 1963, and the essay by Goldmann appended to it. Also Lucien Goldmann's *Pour une Sociologie du Roman*, Gallimard, 1964.
2 See his essay in *La Théorie du Roman*, p. 179.

The difference between a society in which goods are produced as they are needed by those who will use them and one in which goods are produced primarily to be exchanged so as to realize a surplus value is the difference between a world in which men know what they are doing and why (a world of explicit value) and one in which money takes precedence over men, one in which value exists, but implicitly since there is no hope of rationalizing a system in which value becomes ever more remote from what men want and need. Nothing quite makes sense in a culture dominated by exchange value; hence the bourgeois' genius for minimizing the obvious to the advantage of the hidden, his devotion to scientific truth which, since it is given, is inexplicable; hence also his pathetic quest for sincerity in a world of phonies. All of which brings us to a very considerable difficulty which Goldmann himself points out; namely, if an art form is to be regarded as expressing the world view of a class or culture, why should the novel be an exception? How is it that the fictional hero, as Lukacs describes him, far from representing the collective consciousness of the bourgeoisie seems to draw his substance from an opposition, however negative, to it? How can the novel be about an alienation which the bourgeoisie does everything in its power to deny? Or, to put this in another way, why is it that this theory of the problematic hero is almost totally irrelevant to the work of Balzac and Dickens?

It would be difficult to imagine a lapse more serious; and instead of trying to account for it from within the theory (as does Goldmann) we are going to hypothesize the existence of at least two novels. There is the classical novel extending from Balzac to Kafka (excluding the latter); and there is all the rest which we shall loosely call picaresque.

This is, after all, what one would have expected. The difference between Rousseau and Balzac, Fielding and Dickens is one of kind, as is that between the *ancien régime* and modern times. Balzac is still one of us, while even the greatest of the pre-nineteenth-century novels are touched with the quaintness of things belonging to an historical period no longer entirely in focus for us.

The novel is a new form, in fact it did not become fully respectable until well into the last century, and in fighting for its right to be taken seriously it made essentially two claims: it was more 'real' than the literature which preceded it and it had a moral purpose. Let us look first at the realism.

Novelists have always felt obliged to minimize the imaginative content of their stories. We may owe the existence of a novel to the happy discovery of a correspondence or of a diary; or, where the novelist is omniscient, he plies us with detail so painstaking (*Robinson Crusoe*) or offers a view so all-embracing (*La Comédie Humaine*) that we are not inclined to quibble. Even those who loathed reality (Flaubert) were realists; and those who attempted to neglect it to the advantage of the self created the romantic novel—almost a contradiction in terms—which survives only in the classroom. Finally, mass entertainment deals exclusively in 'true life stories'. (It will become increasingly clear that mass entertainment is simply the decaying corpse of the classical novel.)

When a European theatre group performs before an African audience, the Africans (at least in West Africa where I have attended such performances) will tend to laugh through the entire length of the play, no matter how serious or even tragic the subject. I am not sure I can explain this satisfactorily, but a good part of the answer lies surely in African astonishment that people should strive so conscientiously to persuade us of the reality of what we all know is imaginary. Why should an actor trouble to dial a telephone number when everyone knows there is no phone at the other end? Why do anything so absurd unless we are, with all possible accuracy, reconstituting or copying the real so it can be scrutinized with a view to revealing the truth which lies within it? Again we are led to contrast primitive arts of 'event', of the intervention of a beyond, with bourgeois art in which the beyond takes the form of the given, of the 'already present', which one has to decipher.

In chapter nine of his *Anthropologie Structurale*, Lévi-Strauss tells the story of a Zuni Indian boy who was accused of being a sorcerer because a young girl had been taken with a fit of some kind upon having her hands seized by the boy. Brought before tribal judges he at first denied the charge; but then, seeing he was not believed, decided to try a 'confession'. A first attempt to explain how his new power had come to him broke down under the close questioning of the judges. The boy then invented an entirely different account involving a feather which, according to him, was to be found inside a wall of one of the village houses. The wall having been demolished, a feather was indeed found in the rubble and the lad was transformed, as Lévi-Strauss remarks, 'from a threat to the physical security of his group, into a guarantee of its mental coherence'.[3]

The novelist, like the Indian boy, invents stories which will confirm the preconceived notions of his community. There is a vital difference, however; primitive and pre-renaissance art is not art as we understand the word; that is, before the division into the public and private realms, all the major art forms were concerned with the public realm, they were directly metaphysical or sacred, they were able to 'explain' the nature of the universe because that nature was revealed (and not concealed, as for science) in 'secondary' qualities and because it answered the question 'why?' which science disciplined itself into not asking.

But we cannot live without an answer to this question, and the picaresque novel (the novel as defined by Lukacs and Goldmann) is precisely the art form which continues to ask 'why?' even though the only 'valid' answers are no answers at all because given in terms of quantity; that is, they answer the question 'how?'.

The eighteenth-century novel is that of a militantly rationalist bourgeoisie, of a class which had taken up the challenge of making the whole of the real intelligible. In exchange for the sporadic intervention of the beyond, illuminating for simple anthropomorphic reasons a small portion of the real (the seventeenth-century witchcraft trials were the last important manifestation of pre-rationalist attitudes) we have a universal, in-dwelling reason. But universality exacts a heavy price, for whether it is teleological, positivistic, Hegelian, etc., we have a right to ask the question Kierkegaard puts to Hegel: this is all very well, but what about me, what about my unique, personal existence?

In primitive cultures there is always the possibility of an

3 *Anthropologie Structurale*, Plon, 1958, p. 191.

'intervention' to deal with personal problems,[4] while the 'inner world' of our own civilization (for which there is no sensuous access to the beyond) is compelled to 'understand' and this means that, in the last analysis, and paradoxically, it is compelled to have faith—in what is indubitably there, but without our being able to know it. So it is with three of the greatest minds of the period extending from the end of the Renaissance to the French Revolution: for Pascal, God must exist—life would not be possible without him—yet he is no longer 'visible' as he was to a more 'naïve' age; for Hume there is no doubting causality, yet it is extremely difficult to see how we could have knowledge of it; and Kant's philosophy involves the existence of a thing-in-itself which is nevertheless inaccessible to us.[5]

The age of reason is therefore an age of faith; but it is a faith closely bound up with scepticism, especially when questions are asked about daily existence. When this is done— as in the picaresque novel—the results are so grotesque they are often funny. Tom Jones is right to the extent in which he ignores the teaching of Thwackum and Square, the divine and the philosopher, who approve of Blifil the villain of the novel. Voltaire's philosopher Pangloss makes a clown of himself trying to explain to Candide, after each catastrophe, that there was a good reason for it. In his *Neveu de Rameau* Diderot even launches an attack upon that middle-class morality which remains to this day the only 'ethic' of the great free western individual.

The best picaresque fiction then seems to conclude, as a result of its examination of the real, that life does not make all that much sense; in fact its purpose is often to ridicule those who imprudently put forward ideas which obviously will not do. Even the so deferential Wilhem Meister is none too sure. 'The history of his life', we read in book eight, chapter four,

4 See, for example, M. C. Fields's book on mental disturbances among rural Ghanaians, *Search for Security*, Faber and Faber, 1960.

5 The abstentionism of the modern academic and of practically all Anglo-Saxon intellectuals is rooted in this pre-dialectical thought. There is an order about which, unfortunately, nothing can be said (it is being researched) but in which we have faith, otherwise we would be compelled to think about what our society is doing and where it might be going.

'is a perpetual seeking without being able to find'. (A remark Lukacs might have used as an epigraph for his *Theory of the Novel*.)

But we saw that if the novel must be 'real' it must also be 'moral'. No reputable novelist can look upon himself as a storyteller, as an entertainer; except in so far as the 'entertainment' relies for its quality upon the importance of what is being said. The pre-classical novel, therefore, says something important (the *Conte Philosophique*), or it is edifying (Rousseau, Richardson). To be sure, no more important point can be made than the following: 'I may not know what the answers are, but I know at least that *this* is not an answer'; and such, as we have just seen, is the 'message' of the best picaresque.

For increasing numbers of the reading public, however, this would not do; this was not 'serious' literature. Fielding was 'low' for Johnson who turned with relief to the novels of Richardson in which he found the intricacies of the human heart so brilliantly delineated. Such was to be the general direction of the novel, and it is not too difficult to see why. Rationalism rigorously applied will eat into its own substance. It is just as effective against bourgeois morality, justice, equality, etc., as against the absurdities of a feudalism which had long outlived its usefulness. To say, therefore, that the novel is about identity (the 'human heart') is to say that, toward the end of the eighteenth century, it began to shift its attention from the outer world (of which it had failed to make sense) to the inner; and the advantage of so doing is clear: you cannot (at least in the grand manner of the nineteenth century) establish an identity without *taking for granted the existence of a moral order*. So that the passage from the picaresque to the classical novel is marked by the tacit sacrifice of the scepticism of rationalism to its faith. The pitiable sexual morality of Richardson is still, a century later, substantially that of James. Chateaubriand's *Le Génie du Christianisme* opened a campaign of calculated stupidity and obscurantism which is far from closed. The creation of Vautrin and Gobseck is much to Balzac's credit, but their arguments (which are unanswerable, and perhaps because they are unanswerable) worry us far less than those of Rameau's nephew, since Balzac's work rests unspokenly and therefore unshakably upon the 'moral law'.

But this is to anticipate somewhat. The sense in which identity came as the solution to the formal problems of the novel is not yet clear.

We have seen that the novel must be about the real and that it must say something of consequence. To put this more succinctly: *the novel must simultaneously show and tell.* But how? The more accurately the real is shown, the less sense it will make, the less one can 'tell'; the only way to make the real talk, is to give it something to say; but then the novelist is not 'showing reality whole'. This is the dilemma of all nineteenth-century fiction; a dilemma the novelist 'resolved' by seeing in the real a meaning which, with another part of his mind, he knew was not there. Thus western fiction became dedicated to a real to which it remained impervious. The achievement of Dickens in this respect is of course exemplary, and in our own day the film industry photographs a reality which is a waking dream.

If picaresque fiction seems so much more remote to us than does that of Balzac, it is because either what it shows seems pointless or, when the moral is drawn it is done too deliberately. So that at one extreme we have the meaningless adventures of Gil Blas and at the other, the 'unreal' sermons of Rousseau and Richardson. The interminable adventures of the picaresque hero mark the survival of the 'art of event' into an age where event, since it could no longer be an intervention,[6] had to receive its meaning from 'outside'; from the author himself, and hence his unceremonious intrusions into the narrative, the long conversations of master and servant, or Fielding's introductory chapters in *Tom Jones*. In Richardson and Rousseau, the commentary swallows up the event, so that we have more a situation than a narrative; and in any case the letter form although it may admirably reveal the heart, makes it impossible for the reader to be present while things are happening— nothing can be directly shown; so that granting the novelist omniscience seemed a lesser evil than having reality 're-membered in tranquillity' by the letter writer.

---

6 If intervention exists, then it is inscrutable. Wilhem Meister is continually tormented by his ignorance as to whether fate or chance is having the greater influence in his life.

Since the novel must at the same time show and tell, perhaps a solution could be found in presenting a reality the 'showing' of which would in itself constitute a 'telling'. This, as we shall see, was to be Balzac's achievement; but it was attempted prematurely by Scott with the historical novel. If the 'message' of the novel is to be gathered simply from what is shown, then there has to be a consensus about what is being shown, and this existed in the body of romantic illusion about history, chiefly mediaeval. It did not exist in the case of Richardson's transparently vulgar morality; and Rousseau's religiosity had alienated all the major figures of the enlightenment.

Balzac set out in Scott's direction, and his reasons for not continuing are clear enough. When apologists of the novel spoke of the real they meant, of course, the contemporary real. But in any case the historical novelist is confronted by exactly the problem we have mentioned as being that of all non-picaresque fiction: the greater the historical accuracy the greater also the difficulty of saying something of consequence; and the popularity of Scott with educated people necessarily preceded the period of disciplined historical research. There is no great novel which is, properly speaking, an historical novel. The period treated in novels like Balzac's *Les Chouans* or Tolstoy's *War and Peace* was sufficiently close to enable these men to be satisfactorily 'real'. Otherwise the result might be a work like *Salammbô* in which Flaubert is so 'accurate' he is obliged to replace the indispensable message of fiction with aestheticism, thus producing a book some critics are reluctant to regard as a novel at all. Since Flaubert, of course, we have realized that a culture is not only a peculiar material apparatus, but a mentality of which we can have little conception; so that historical fiction is now produced solely for the undiscerning since rubbish of that sort, we are told, is what the 'people want'.

The problem remained, consequently, of finding a reality suitable for 'reproduction' in the novel; a reality, that is, the mere showing of which would be, without the aid of nudging from the author, a serious commentary upon life. If, in other words, the classical novel, as we maintain, expresses the *vision du monde* of the bourgeoisie, there must have existed a social reality about which there was widespread agreement. Yet how

could this be since the very word 'bourgeois' is a term of abuse?
The worth of a nineteenth-century writer or thinker can be
measured very accurately by the depth of his contempt for
bourgeois civilization. Uncritical acceptance—today as then—
is the infallible mark of mediocrity. The finest achievement of
scientific rationalism is perhaps its disinterested intellectual
curiosity to which, ideally, it sets no bounds. But if 'free inquiry'
has been unable to alter in any essential way a society whose
real values (as opposed to its spoken ones) are held in
universal contempt, it is because there is a place for free inquiry
within the system. Given the divorce between the public and
private realms, the true function of free inquiry is to aid in the
construction of a noble and intelligent self since the public
realm (being that of science, chance, fate, God's will, etc.) is,
by definition, separate.

Nevertheless the nineteenth-century reading public could
not have rejoiced in the sometimes deeply felt criticism of its
way of life to be found in Balzac, Flaubert, Dickens, or Zola;
and if these authors were so widely and often so enthusiastically
read, it could only be because they offered something their
readers were looking for and could use. Whatever it was, it
will be beyond the reach of free inquiry which belongs to the
explicit level of the novel's message (Balzac on the evils of
money, Dickens on debtors' prisons, etc.). It will be expressed,
if not quite unconsciously, at least implicitly; and it had to
be implicit because its function was to permit the bourgeoisie
to comfort itself in a manner which had nothing to do with its
declared political ideology. I am referring, of course, to the
notion of identity, and if we examine some remarks Rousseau
makes in *La Nouvelle Héloïse* my meaning will be perfectly clear.

The heroine of this novel—Julie—is of noble birth, and her
father will not allow her to marry Saint-Preux who is not.
Rousseau impresses upon the reader that the continued refusal
of Julie's father is both unenlightened and (in the circumstances) almost criminal. And yet relations between Julie,
Saint-Preux, Wolmar and the peasants who have come to
help with the harvest are as follows: 'We do not, with mis-
placed pride, sneer at their awkward air and gross compli-
ments; to put them at their ease we unaffectedly fall in with
their ways. This complaisance does not escape them . . . and

seeing that we are prepared to quit our station for their sake, they are the more content to remain in their own' (Part V, letter 7, Garnier, 1960, pages 594–5). On the very next page this is described as the reign of a *douce égalité*; and perhaps anticipating our surprise Rousseau explains that social intercourse of such a kind '. . . re-established the natural order . . .'. The attitude of Julie's father was the consequence of an aristocratic prejudice, whereas that of Saint-Preux towards the peasants was the result of objective 'knowledge' of the order of nature from which identity is derived. The peasants were not inferior, they were simply a different kind of people; and so it was to be with the working class down to our own time.[7]

Rameau's nephew exclaims at one point: 'Damned if I know what I really am at bottom', and this is a remark we could all echo. Fielding refuses to 'identify' Tom Jones, who is neither good nor bad. But the classical novel could never have come into being had such a view prevailed. Julie speaks of her husband as having a 'supernatural gift for reading people's hearts' (Part 4, letter 12) and in the following letter it is said: '. . . we may be confused as to our state if we give it no thought, but as soon as our attention is turned upon it we see it as it is, and it is no more possible to deceive ourselves about our virtues than about our vices'. Thus there can be self-knowledge and, by extension, knowledge of others. This principle is the substance of the classical novel, and yet the futility of introspection is there to demonstrate its absurdity. But we know how much was to be gained, and we can already sense what it was in *La Nouvelle Héloïse* since Rousseau says of Julie that she shows an 'exquisite discernment in apportioning her aid to the needy, either in her choice of the means of being useful, or in her choice of the people who are to receive help' (Part 5, letter 2). How dare she take it upon herself to 'discern'? She could only do so on the basis of infallible, God-like know-

---

7 There are, of course, many other eighteenth-century texts from which we can learn what the bourgeois meant and still means (in so far as he still thinks about anything at all) by 'equality'. In Sedaine's play *Le Philosophe sans le Savoir* (Act II, Scene 4) the father explains to his son that there are only two callings he would set above that of the merchant: 'Assuming that there is any difference between men who do the best they know how in whatever rank heaven has placed them'. There is no difference between men, they simply occupy different ranks!

ledge, and once the possibility of such 'knowledge' is granted we have a pretext for those wholesale exclusions of lesser breeds to which bourgeois culture is so very prone.

That there should be knowledge of people, that we should be presumed, in other words, to have an identity is what enabled Balzac to create the classical novel. This is the 'reality' which is in itself a moral lesson. We need not be told how dangerous or undesirable it is to be a Grandet, a Hulot, or a Lucien de Rubempré; it is sufficient that they be 'shown' to us; and the economic, social and political realities which may also be shown are simply the milieu in which such identities would naturally be found, and in which they are confirmed.

It may be said of the picaresque novel, both historical and contemporary (each in its own way, of course, since a century separates them), that it interrogates reality, while classical fiction shows it; the one asks questions, the other makes statements. The formlessness of the novel is often remarked upon, but this is because critics have not known what the novel was about. As soon as the novel, with Balzac, found in identity a reality all its own, it ceased to be formless. One could demonstrate the 'necessity' (a necessity to be sure much less rigorous than that to be found in more formal art like painting or music) of almost every paragraph in a book like *Eugénie Grandet;* for Balzac is either (in his descriptive passages) setting forth the identity of old Grandet as a given or, where he narrates, this given is proven through all of Grandet's actions. I will be accused of confounding form and content since identity is what classical fiction is about, as a painting is 'about' a landscape, its aesthetic value depending upon the manner in which the subject is treated. But this, precisely, is indispensable to any satisfactory definition of fiction: the fact that here, much more so than in any other art, content and form are inextricable. Hence the historical interest of Flaubert who tried to extricate them; hence also the superficiality of a book like Lubbock's *The Craft of Fiction.* Fiction is not a craft, it is a statement or an interrogation.

Returning to *Eugénie Grandet,* the statement (which will be implicit, as opposed to the explicit denunciation of the omnipotence of money) takes the form of another identity, that of Eugénie herself. We saw that if the novelist were to be able to show and tell simultaneously, there would have to be some general agreement. This agreement is reached over Eugénie's 'goodness' and, by implication, the 'badness' of the characters who have least in common with her. However, even among Balzac's contemporaries there were certainly some who would have seen in Eugénie less a 'saint' than a victim of the 'idiocy of country life'. Nevertheless, agreement would still have existed (practically universal this time) over the *unchangeability* of Eugénie's goodness; in other words, over identity as a given. This is the 'necessity' mentioned a moment ago; one need only try to imagine Eugénie doing a vile thing or Grandet giving a large sum of money to a charity to appreciate that in identity as a given we have the one element absolutely indispensable to the existence of classical fiction as such. This is structural as opposed to scientific necessity. Balzac would have been free to have Eugénie do something immoral, but at the cost of making his novel incomprehensible.

We saw how the separation of value and explanation served— and serves—a purpose, in what sense bourgeois rationalism is a praxis. We also saw that the novel as 'congealed' praxis, as *pratico-inerte*, has a 'life of its own' in that, having failed to show and tell simultaneously, it 'needed' Balzac's introduction of identity as the basic structure of the classical novel. And yet mysteriously this was at the same time exactly what the bourgeoisie as a class required; for identity *reconciles explanation and value*. But necessarily it does so only on the implicit level where it can escape too close a scrutiny since for the classical rationalist one cannot observe objectively (show) and simultaneously make value judgments (tell). The scepticism which, as we saw, is built into rationalism was relegated to the explicit level of the novel where it could do little harm since from Flaubert onward it was seen to detract not only from the aesthetic value of the work, but also from its practical effect; for a judgment coming too overtly from the author himself could only be 'one man's opinion'; that is, a 'subjective distortion'.

With the spreading of the factory system it became at once more essential and more impossible to genuinely reconcile explanation and value. The great nineteenth-century realists were in the position of having to deplore the terrible social abuses of their day, while adopting precisely that attitude of detached observation which made the abuses possible but which was taken to be the only means of arriving at an explanation.

In the classical novel, therefore, the bourgeoisie has it both ways. Implicitly, it makes statements and passes judgments (since an identity is always good or bad, desirable or undesirable) and it does so necessarily (since the statement is implicit) on the basis of bourgeois morality. On the other hand, explicit criticism and opposition, however virulent, in fact *because* it is virulent, will detract from the novel both as a work of art and as an impartial 'scientific' view of reality.

Let us see how these difficulties were dealt with by some of the nineteenth-century's greatest novelists.

4 Balzac, Flaubert, Zola, Stendhal

On ne devient ici-bas que ce qu'on est.
Splendeurs et Misères des Courtisanes

In his *Aspects of the Novel* (Arnold, 1960) Forster notes on page 61, referring to character, that we get from the novel: '. . . a reality of a kind we can never get in daily life'; and on page 62: '. . . fiction is truer than history because it goes beyond the evidence, and each of us knows from his experience that there is something beyond the evidence . . .''. But there is nothing beyond except what we put there to fulfil one of the basic needs of bourgeois culture—the need to identify so that the atomism of our society can be given a semblance of order, so that the unique and distinguished 'I' can continue to relate itself to principle rather than to the vulgar 'we' which produced it.

The novel (and it will be remembered we are dealing exclusively with the classical novel) is certainly about character, since even great novels seem to be able to dispense with almost everything else. They can be badly written and organized, devoid of wisdom, in fact negative in every respect but this. We do not read a novel to know what is going to happen next, but to know what is going to happen to a person identified as this or that, or whose identity is not yet revealed. Otherwise many newspaper accounts would be novels.

Forster does well to suggest that we learn from the novel; but what we learn from the explicit is not compelling and the implicit message is one we already know, one we need, one which endlessly reiterates (in mass entertainment in particular) the existence of order. The novel is not about order itself—this is the domain of science and philosophy—it is about the way in which order manifests itself in daily life. The classical novel is 'instructive' in the sense that it always ends appropriately; its 'statement' consists in showing that, given this identity, an ending of this sort inevitably follows.

68

If, however, we are to be sure that an ending is appropriate we must be sure that there has been no change of identity; and therefore in the classical novel *no change of identity ever occurs* (otherwise of course it could not be a given). What can happen, is the concealment of identity for a greater or lesser period. These notions are of the utmost importance and must be carefully examined.

There is something of the Promethean romantic hero in Balzac's great men; for while it is suggested by the romantics that the poet, like De Vigny's Chatterton, points the way for mankind, the all-important message never gets expressed, so that the divine spark is in reality a divine self to which the gross herd remains insensible and which it may even martyr. The genius in Balzac's novels can be a scientist or a philosopher as well as a poet, and Balzac will usually insist upon the necessity for long hard work (whereas the romantic might find 'inspiration' sufficient) and yet for Balzac as for the romantic, genius is *primarily an endowment,* a given, which years of labour simply confirm. In his descriptions of Paris, Balzac will often stop to exclaim over the number of men who, hungry and cold, may be toiling away in the garrets of the city, men whose work may alter the fate of humanity; men *already great,* in other words, though as yet unknown. Hegel had said that one could not be a poet without writing poetry; and yet for Balzac, greatness is there long before it manifests itself, and in *Les Illusions Perdues* we meet a whole group of future great men, men in whose faces and bearing there is the mark of an election.

What is this novel about? Explicitly Balzac is saying that in a society such as ours, one in which men are the things of money rather than the reverse, not only will women have to prostitute their bodies, men will have to prostitute their minds. There is a market for literature as for everything else, so that to succeed you must furnish a product for which there is a demand. The realization that the poet must sell himself to live is what destroys Lucien's illusions. In brief *Les Illusions Perdues* is about what almost all of Balzac's best novels are about: the evil which ensues when the value of money supplants all other values. If this is what Balzac is 'telling', then it becomes nonsensical to regard the novel as the supreme art form of bourgeois culture.

But there remains the implicit level of discourse on which Balzac is saying something very different indeed; something his readers were grateful to hear, something in fact which annuls to a great extent the explicit message of *La Comédie Humaine*. For what really defeats Lucien de Rubempré is not bourgeois society at all but the possession of a 'wrong' identity. His suicide is simply the confirmation of an identity made clear to the reader the moment Lucien is introduced several volumes earlier. He is weak, he yields continually to facility and temptation and he is consequently marked for destruction. Inversely, Bianchon is inhabited by a greatness at present hidden but which will and must come eventually to light.

This extraordinary contradiction (characteristic of almost all nineteenth-century fiction) appears most flagrantly perhaps in Balzac's short novel *Gobseck*. Gobseck points out irrefutably and at length that the 'modern God' is money, to own money is to own men and women, the law exists to protect the wealth of the rich and to enable them to acquire it through 'lawful theft' etc., etc. Gobseck then recounts his visit to a certain Sophie Malvaut whom he describes as leading a 'pure and solitary life'; there was an 'indefinable air of virtue about her'; and Gobseck exclaims: 'Poor innocent creature! there were things she believed in.' Yet how could Gobseck use such a vocabulary ('pure', 'virtue', 'innocent' . . .) unless he also believed? In real life, to be sure, such language would be expressive merely of nostalgia perhaps, or sympathy for Sophie Malvaut as a person, and so forth. But in the classical novel identity is a *given;* it is the moral order rendered visible. Sophie's virtue is in her face for everyone to see; and, as in the case of Eugénie, it is unthinkable that she do or say a vile thing.

We are left then with that astonishing mentality which, obliged to believe in nothing 'unconsciously' compels itself to believe in everything. The bourgeois individual shows forth in his property, culture, self-respect and general distinction of manner an order about which he can tell us nothing without appearing ridiculous, or without falling into 'metaphysics'. For the supreme expression of value in a valueless universe one must attend a lecture on the absurd in contemporary literature given by a product of the English public school Oxbridge system. Such a person will have been equipped with an identity which is unchangeably given (since it is revealed in accent, gesture, and mannerism) which therefore involves (as in the novel) an implicit statement of value; and yet that identity will be used to proclaim the meaninglessness of the world we live in.

When the western intellectual speaks of the absurd he refers as always to a given of which he has knowledge; and the having of such knowledge constitutes the demonstration of an identity to which the 'masses' can lay no claim. In rather the same way, Vautrin's attack upon bourgeois values is conducted from the inside. His 'opposition' actually reinforces the regime for which he professes contempt, since despite his clear recognition of its murderous hypocrisy the whole purpose of his life is to gain readmission to a society from which (since he possessed a 'correct' identity) he had been unjustly excluded. In this he succeeds for he terminates his career working for the police! In exactly the same way, the western intellectual who has (or should have) a loathing for what colonialism and neo-colonialism is doing in the backward parts of the world, nevertheless actually supports this exploitation since, though he is aware of the facts, they are not sufficient to drive him to organized resistance. In view of the growing desperateness of the world situation, the intellectual can justify his 'objective' abstention only in so far as he accepts some form of nineteenth-century scientism; just as Vautrin's 'hatred' for his society coexisted with a full implicit acceptance of the Christian order.

I have referred several times to hidden identity in the novel; Vautrin offers an excellent opportunity to go into this matter more thoroughly.

Vautrin is the arch-criminal of *La Comédie Humaine,* and if he eventually comes to be employed by the police this surely involves a change of identity which destroys my thesis. (Balzac unfortunately is not suggesting that between criminals and the police there is often precious little to choose, for in the concluding section of *Splendeurs et Misères des Courtisanes* he is clearly as much a police and prison enthusiast as Dickens himself.) Partly, of course, the answer is that Vautrin is not altogether the same character in all the novels in which he figures; Balzac used him depending upon the exigencies of the moment. Nevertheless there is sufficient continuity for the appearance of a problem to exist. It is no more than an appearance, however; for, like Balzac himself, Vautrin was wed to his society with the whole affectivity of his being, so that his love for Rastignac and Lucien de Rubempré was in large part a love of the life they led from which he was excluded, but which he could in this way enjoy at least by proxy. I am not sure that Balzac is anywhere specific as to Vautrin's origin, but in the play *Vautrin*, it is said of Vautrin's accomplices in crime that '*they* did not fall'; in other words, Vautrin was not born in the mileu. In *Le Père Goriot* we learn that Vautrin's first prison term was one he voluntarily incurred so as to spare someone else the ordeal. Vautrin has many admirable qualities—courage, resourcefulness, loyalty; his 'evil' is almost all in his talk. Finally, his love for Lucien survives even the latter's suicide, and turns out to be so deep that Vautrin undergoes a sort of crisis proof of identity and loses even the appearance of criminality.

We have seen that, with identity as a given, the novel discovered a means of showing reality and simultaneously commenting upon it, interpeting it, conveying a morality, and so forth; and all this could be done implicitly, so that the 'showing' would be that much more convincing, even 'scientific' perhaps. But also, the showing of identity is a praxis enabling bourgeois society to justify itself in its own eyes; for if, as we have just seen, it is not really society which destroys Lucien de Rubempré, but his lack of an identity which would have enabled him to survive, then by implication, the persistence of all the ills known to man and the aggravation of some of them despite the coming of liberty, equality and fraternity is not to be attributed to any failing or inadequacy in the new social order. Once again, and as always, it is a question of *kinds of people*; so that if the poor continue to lead lives of frightful privation it is because 'the poor will always be with us'; because, given people of this identity, then this must follow. Increase wages or shorten the working day and all you get is even more immorality in the mill towns.

But surely some injustice is done? Surely children sometimes starve without having brought it upon themselves through their ingrained corruption? The novel concedes this, but the explanation is a simple one: it is possible (though very rare) as the result of an unusual concatenation of circumstances (hence it is a story 'worth telling') for a good identity to become so obscured that people are understandably mistaken about it as in the case of Vautrin, Lorenzaccio, Jean Valjean, Camille, little Nell, Oliver Twist, and a whole population of others down to Superman.

In general, however, this device belongs to the lower reaches of fiction, and Vautrin is far more important as an expression of the explicit in Balzac than as a case of mistaken identity. But then how does Balzac deal with the problem of the persecution of the good[1] if he refuses to believe that it is simply a matter of its going unrecognized?

The answer is that the good are not of this world and consequently cannot be touched by it. They are those people who, alone in the *Comédie Humaine*, are totally unaffected by the evil of money. This is one of the means by which Balzac makes the explicit in his work more telling than it would otherwise have been, for a good identity is proven not only through reference to the Christian beyond, but by its revulsion from a society in which money is the only genuine value. Characters like Colonel Chabert, Eugénie Grandet, Véronique Graslin, etc., want no part of such a world and their unhappy lives are therefore in a sense chosen. Virtue is its own reward.

The real problem for Balzac was not to explain why a good identity should be no protection against great unhappiness. In fact there was no problem for Balzac, but an absolute contradiction; and his refusal to resolve it by attenuating the explicit content of his work is a good part of his greatness as a novelist. The contradiction is this: if we accept Balzac's denunciation of our society for having made of money the supreme and only value (and he is unremitting in this) then success is incompatible with the proving of a good identity. Lesser novelists, when they faced the issue at all, wriggled out by hypocritically defining success as an income sufficient for the enjoyment of the simple, honest and inexpensive pleasures

---

1 There is of course no problem of the persecution of the 'good'. This is an example of the way in which a culture will phrase its questions so as to get the answers it wants. If there are good and bad people there has to be a beyond to guarantee these identities; and it will also, no doubt, see to it that justice is done, if not in this life then in the next.

of country life. Balzac yields here and there to this temptation, but for the most part he is uncompromising: there is no life apart from success and to be successful was to be acceptable in the highest regions of Parisian society; but without a very considerable fortune this was quite unthinkable.

No one achieves any worthwhile success without doing violence to his fellows according to Vautrin. The only choice is between legal violence (that of the rich banker Nucingen, for example) or the overt violence of Vautrin himself. Even though the killing of a man in a duel is involved, there are no strictly rational grounds on which Rastignac can reject Vautrin's scheme for acquiring a fortune very quickly; and if, finally, he does so, it is simply because he is not that 'kind of person' (Balzac continually refers to him as a 'superior' man, even though, as in the case of his unknown 'great men', we never find Rastignac *doing* anything superior, quite the contrary) or, as Rastignac puts it: 'I don't want to think about anything, the heart is a good guide'.[2] If the 'outer world' fails to make sense, there is always the 'moral law within'. Why then does not everyone abide by the moral law? Because everyone is not equipped with a 'heart' of the right kind, because there is '. . . the great question of temperament which, whatever people say, dominates society'.[3]

Rastignac does without Vautrin's help but succeeds nevertheless; so that success does not inevitably rule out a correct identity. Balzac, however, does not face the issue squarely since Rastignac has the invaluable help of his cousin Madame de Beauséant.

Dostoevsky goes further since his Raskolnikov commits the crime from which Rastignac's identity is able to save him, and this occurs because Raskolnikov is in himself both Vautrin and Rastignac. With Dostoevsky (and, as we shall see, with Stendhal) there begins that disintegration of identity which will destroy the classical novel. We have seen that, in our culture, belief is both impossible and compulsory, and that in the classical novel this contradiction is dealt with by asserting belief implicitly through identity. Dostoevsky drags this sub-

2 *Le Père Goriot*, Livre de Poche, p. 186.
3 *Ibid.*, p. 220.

terfuge into the open by demanding that we make an honest choice: it must be either crime, individual or collective (revolution), which can always be justified from a purely rational point of view; or we must admit that reason is not enough and fall back upon religion, not in the hypocritical form of kinds of people, but as a whole way of life. The beauty of characters like Prince Myshkin and Alyosha is that they do not judge; they are not 'good' as are the good in Balzac or Dickens who exist so that the 'bad' may also be discerned. In *The Brothers Karamazov* there is a chapter entitled 'The Rebellion' (far superior to 'The Great Inquisitor' immediately following it which has received so much more attention) in which Alyosha is shaken to realize that if to kill is a crime, doing nothing is also a crime; it is the bourgeois crime par excellence, that of nice people, crime by default, crime that leaves the hands clean. Identity places the debate upon much safer grounds: the real issue then becomes not what is done or not done but who you are. Myshkin refuses *to be* since one arrives at a favourable self-definition only by seeking deficiences in others. To identify another is always an aggressive act, the transformation of an effort or a direction into an object; and yet to refuse to do so is to risk, like Myshkin, being taken for an 'idiot', being taken for one lacking the most elementary knowledge of others.[4]

The greatest danger a novelist faces is that of falling into triviality since his is a 'non-sacred' art; or, more exactly, the sacred is driven underground, it is implicit. Triviality is most successfully avoided (as in Balzac) where the novelist is not afraid of the doubt in rationalism and succeeds in expressing it without turning his fiction into tracts for the times. The vast majority of nineteenth-century novelists, however, took just the opposite course, they suppress the doubt altogether, and bring the implicit as close to the surface as possible. In this

4 Characters like the father in *The Brothers Karamazov* and the hero of *Letters from the Underworld* are especially striking examples of the disintegration of identity which, perhaps more than any other single factor, gives Dostoevsky's work its profundity, and its appeal for our time. Much of contemporary literature sets forth, in one form or another, this dilemma: on the one hand consciousness is alienated in the self; and on the other, to be unable to live with this socially imposed self (the loathsome respectable self of bourgeois individualism) is to incur ridicule or hatred.

way triviality is 'avoided' through sensationalism which consists in showing how the beyond regulates life by opportunely and infallibly adjusting events in view of the identities involved. Thus the bullet of the cowboy hero (or the sword of d'Artagnan) unerringly finds its mark thanks not to the weapon itself (there can be no excalibur revolvers, as this would be sacred art) nor to chance, nor to anything but the goodness of the hero and the badness of his enemies.

Since the beyond functions infallibly the reader's interest has to be 'artificially' maintained and, generally, this is done in one of two ways: identity is concealed from both the reader and the other characters (detective novel) or it is revealed to the reader but not to other characters. Where it is clear to everyone from the outset, as is usually the case in Dickens and Balzac, then other factors come into play—the explicit in Balzac, humour in Dickens.[5]

Once again then we are confronted by a formal requirement (necessity of avoiding triviality) which is at the same time an aspect of a social praxis since, as we have seen, concealed identity accounts for the suffering of the innocent in a society which had abolished that sort of thing, or at least would shortly do so. We already know, however, that this by no means exhausts the resourcefulness of identity as an alibi, as an instrument of class rule, for the bourgeois needs desperately to believe that the public realm (which has been turned over to the anarchy necessary to private enterprise) is no responsibility of his, and when things go wrong it is because certain individuals, evil by nature, have striven to bring this about. Hence our obsessive interest in crime and criminals. Social problems may be eliminated by eliminating certain individuals.

---

5 There is also the possibility that identity be dealt with so subtly—both in the nature of the identities in question, and the manner in which they are withheld or revealed—that the sensationalism just mentioned is avoided. Such is the case with Jane Austen. In *Pride and Prejudice*, for example, the identities of Wickham and Darcy are exactly the opposite of what they initially appear to be; and the attention of Jane Austen's readers (but not necessarily that of the scholar—we shall return to this issue in the chapter on Dickens) centred upon the way in which the reversal, after many indications and counter-indications, is slowly brought about. (Not without, it is true, a certain amount of sensationalism given the placidity of the lives the characters usually led.)

George Eliot (*Felix Holt*) and Dickens (*Hard Times*) warned their readers that union organizers (and not starvation) were fomenting discontent among the workers; and similarly, today, the James Bond books and films indicate that we propose to deal with global problems in the same way—not by eliminating starvation, but by eliminating criminal types, and this pursuit easily becomes a 'crusade'. It is therefore not surprising it should be the Great Society which tried to annihilate the peoples and cultures of Vietnam.

How easily we fail to notice, in one of Madame de Beauséant's conversations with Rastignac, that social problems are—absurdly—being dealt with in terms of good and bad individuals. She explains, in the manner of Vautrin, that to succeed in our society is to comport oneself in a way ill-befitting a human being, let alone a Christian. She then invites Rastignac to make use of her name, for it will be of great help to him, but he is enjoined to see that it remains 'spotless'. Madame de Beauséant, consequently, although she is a pillar of the loathsome social order she had described is not part of it at all; and this miracle of separateness she owes to her identity; or, more exactly, to the fact she can find 'within herself' only intentions which are pure.

The bourgeois ethic of intention is a wondrous device and deserves far more lengthy a discussion than we can give it here. The violence of bourgeois society is often concealed because no one intends it, it just somehow happens; and overt violence is, in nineteenth-century fiction, a sure indication of defective identity. Hence the good in Balzac (his women at least) and Dickens never riposte, whatever the provocation. This passivity of the good, however, would seem to involve us in a contradiction, since it is certainly not characteristic of contemporary mass entertainment; and if our theory is valid (making use, as it does, of both Marxism and structuralism) then this entertainment must be seen to be the high bourgeois art of the last century adapting itself as best it can to the requirements of the moment.

The difficulty may be put in the following way: we have seen that the nineteenth-century novel expresses implicitly much that would be inadmissible for the rationalism it deploys, sometimes noisily, on the explicit level; and that it was for the reassuring nature of its implicit content that this fiction was so widely read and appreciated. In the films and stories of the present day, to be sure, the villain continues to be brought to justice and the good rewarded. But it would seem that much of this literature is consumed for its sex and violence rather than for the implicit comfort it provides. The question is worth stopping for.

The return to 'picaresque' fiction which comes early in the present century is quite simply the separation of the explicit and the implicit in the classical novel; it is the end of an ambiguity which had become intolerable. The 'explicit' (this terminology is valid of course only for the classical novel) becomes an interrogation[6]—the questioning of a tiny élite partially alienated from its own culture—while the implicit expands unchecked into sensationalism. Contemporary sensationalism, however, is far more vicious and prurient in nature than that of, say, the Victorian melodrama, and it would appear to exist for its own sake, whereas in the melodrama it was simply the 'pretext' for the last-minute rescue of the heroine.

The problem is to some extent an invented one because literature relying upon gratuitous sadism existed throughout the nineteenth century. The change comes with the enormous improvements in techniques of printing and illustrating along with, of course, the generalization of literacy. Traffic will fill the roads provided for it, and similarly our means of producing and disseminating sub-literature will never outstrip the supply.

A new technique, however, explains little; the question, as we know now, must always be 'why?'—why do men use this technique in this particular way, what do they 'intend' by its use? The generalization of literacy accompanies the gradual

6 Most students (and, unfortunately, no negligible number of critics) will try to interpret Gide's *l'Immoraliste* as though it were a classical novel; that is, they assume Gide was copying that moralized reality which is identity in classical fiction. The book then becomes an objective record of how the hero's evil identity gradually emerged. Gide's preface to this novel and innumerable indications in the text itself are powerless against the average student's comfortable adjustment to his class and society which he betrays in assuming that he has come to the university to pursue knowledge of writers like Gide who are considered to be doing exactly the same thing with their fictional characters.

improvement in working-class standards of living which came at the end of the last century and the result has been the creation of a vast amorphous ever-growing class of people who have lost the solidarity of the old working-class community without acquiring the security which the established bourgeoisie owes to its wealth and culture. To become literate for the working-class child could only mean to accede to 'individualism'; he could then, in theory, improve himself; but in the overwhelming majority of cases he had simply become exposed to the hidden violence of our society with the protection neither of a collectivity nor of the 'personal distinction' which belongs to those debarred from none of the privileges their society affords.

Contempt and hatred for the masses is the life blood of western individualism. To be educated is to have contracted a terror of anonymity from which we escape by being 'original', 'thinking for ourselves', and rejecting the 'values of the herd'. But as we have seen, identity is not *created* by what we do, it is *confirmed* by it; so that, fortunately for everyone, *genuine* independence of any kind is not required. On the contrary, it is by conforming to certain generally accepted forms of display that an identity is confirmed. And so we arrive at that extraordinary product of our culture, the elaborately conforming free individual.

The disease of individualism is self-contempt. If man is initiative (praxis) and nothing more, and yet if his only freedom—as in our society—is that of self-confirmation, then he is free only to thwart and frustrate himself. For to be free in any true sense is to be able to *change reality*. But this is not practicable apart from collective enterprise (in which the individual is fearful of being 'swallowed up') unless the change is in reality simply the emerging of the hidden violence of our society; of that violence which, having no legal or ideological justification, is said to be in the nature of things. When the system is threatened (as it has been since 1917 by communism), it erects its violence into an 'ideology', and this we call fascism. Communist violence is directed primarily against the environment, against things; and it falls upon men only in so far as they constitute (or are thought, or are said to constitute) obstacles to the realization of environmental changes. Fascist violence

79

as we would expect—since our culture poses all its problems in terms of good or bad individuals—is directed against men themselves, and is therefore inseparable from racism in one form or another.[7] Racism serves two purposes: it enables a government in times of difficulty to take action without touching the social and economic structure, and it wins support for its 'program' by offering a distinction accessible to practically all since it consists simply in not being a Jew, a Negro, a communist, etc.

Apart from its talk, literature, and propaganda, our society offers *one* 'ideal', that of self-aggrandizement and display usually through a wealth far beyond the reach of the great majority of the people. To be culturally part of a society from which you are nevertheless *excluded* is to suffer a self-hatred which, notoriously, will be dealt with by hatred of others. But this hatred must remain unavowed, since people are afflicted with it precisely because they have accepted the bourgeois moral order which protects us from the 'anarchy' of revolutionary praxis. Our violence, consequently, has to be 'morally justified' violence; whether it be that of the fascist warning us against various 'international conspiracies', or of the white man beleaguered by blacks and trying to 'protect his women' and his 'civilization'.

These then are the general considerations which I think will serve best to account for the degeneration of the classical novel into present-day mass entertainment. The explicit content of the former becomes a new picaresque; that is, opposition invents new forms (contemporary art in its entirety) with which to combat a despised culture while the implicit content of the classical novel remains (identity as a given-proven) but emphasis shifts from the *fact* that an identity is always proven, to the *manner in which* it is proven—to the supreme and infallible violence with which the hero overcomes the violence

7 Nationalism would be one such form (although a 'negative' one), and it is obviously characteristic of communism in its present stage. We can, however, see its usefulness in countries struggling out of illiteracy, starvation and colonial humiliation, whereas in Gaullist France it is pitiable. There is undoubtedly anti-semitism in Russia, but the authorities deny it; in other words, it is held to be incompatible with socialism. In the west it is taken for granted, for wherever the private realm is paramount, racism will be the cheapest and easiest means of maintaining it.

of which he is the innocent victim. The glass-eyed residents of suburbia are the dumb collective victims of a violence to which they are able to respond only as individuals. Their art consequently individualizes violence (mad scientists, communist conspirators, criminals, etc.) so that it may be countered by individuals whether Superman, or the heroes of films like Kazan's *Viva Zapata* and *On the Waterfront* or, for the absolutely adult, there are books like Camus's *l'Homme Révolté* in which a temporary 'we' is allowed (revolt) on condition that success (revolution) is not envisaged since this leads to tyranny. We are therefore conveniently blocked at our own moment of history.[8]

FLAUBERT

We have seen that the problem of the classical novel was to convey a moral by simply 'copying reality'. Flaubert worked out a 'solution' which was to enjoy great popularity down to the publication of Sartre's *What is Literature?*, and beyond. Art *is* morality, he claimed; in fact the only morality is art, so there is no problem.

It follows at once that the explicit in fiction, often so obtrusive in Balzac, can be safely dropped, for the novel no longer has anything to say. The novelist is no longer, as Balzac remarked in his *Avant-Propos* for the *Comédie Humaine*, quoting Bonald, a 'teacher of men'. Or, to express this differently, the explicit in the novel is its 'beauty'; the novelist passes reality through the crucible of his prose until there is left only that quintessence

8 If popular culture were our immediate concern many other suggestions might be made. What, for example, is the reason for the striking insistence with which the public is assured that its various entertainment idols lead lives which, in all essential respects, are exactly those of everyone else? The implication, I think, is that these people prove an identity thanks to physical appearance alone (or to some commonplace 'talent') with the result that their fans are able to consider themselves examples of hidden identity. Hence the innumerable interviews with cinema stars reported in magazines and newspapers from which we learn of their hopes and fears, their tastes and thoughts which, since they are all but indistinguishable from our own, indicate in ourselves an exceptional identity, though unhappily it may never be revealed because we are ugly or have had bad luck. The handsome ciphers of the cinema (and more generally the idle rich) lead lives to which *we* are entitled; so that there lies just beneath the surface of our society a vast reservoir of resentment, of overlooked or neglected 'merit' ready for use by political conservatism.

which is beauty. Balzac himself is to be looked for perhaps in Vautrin more than in any of his other characters, for Vautrin is undeservedly excluded from a society he yearns to have at his feet. Instead, he lords it over the underworld, as Balzac was the master of the society of his time, but only in imagination. Balzac's opposition was impurely flecked with envy. Could it not be argued therefore that Flaubert restores to rationalism the full strength of its inherent scepticism? He believes in neither God nor science but only in a quality—beauty—which the bourgeois destroys in everything he alters and excludes from everything he constructs.

Can showing and telling be successfully reconciled in this way?—by saying that showing is in itself telling provided the novelist understands that the 'moral' emerges from reality itself in the form of beauty, and that beauty is the highest protest since it removes the debate to a realm inaccessible to the bourgeois? To the clanking utilitarianism of the industrious middle-classes we will oppose the gratuity of art, and of all criticism this is the profoundest.

Unfortunately it is not possible to say nothing in prose (even the politician or logical positivist is eloquent by what he omits or cannot see) so that Flaubert survives for what, despite himself, he tells his readers. But since the explicit level of discourse has been suppressed, (or become beauty, whichever one prefers. In any case the explicit will be largely ignored, as it was in Balzac. Flaubert was not for his public a great aesthete, but 'the father of French realism'). In other words, since Flaubert makes it a matter of principle never to speak as an *individual* subjectivity, he implicitly voices with unrivalled clarity the *cultural* subjectivity of a social class. Flaubert's total opposition resolves itself, in his art, into total conformism. Let us look at this in greater detail.

In Part IV, letter eleven, of *La Nouvelle Héloïse*, Wolmar explains to Saint-Preux how a pleasure garden had been planned, created, and then all trace of human interference removed. This incident wonderfully symbolizes bourgeois culture which creates the world we live in while maintaining it all comes from God or that it is to be understood in terms of 'natural law'; either way it has nothing to do with any merely human wish or endeavour. Such is 'reality' as Flaubert presents it to us; the result of a long elaborate enterprise engaged in by no one; a vision of the world divorced from any particular seeing eye. One of Wolmar's purposes, presumably, was to render more plainly visible the wonderful teleology of God. Flaubert also assists nature to express herself, but in common with much nineteenth- and twentieth-century 'atheism', he finds the message a more sobering one than any the eighteenth century had received. There is in Flaubert a 'reverse teleology' which makes of human desire a romantic aberration. But if reality is to thwart us systematically in this way, it cannot be the inert, measured reality of science; so that in order to introduce it Flaubert is obliged *to widen the area of implicit expression.* Instead of identifying individuals by a more or less overt reference to Christian values, Flaubert identifies humanity as a whole by reference to an implacable and at times even sardonic reality. Men are no longer so much good or bad in a variety of ways, as simply futile and foolish. From this wretched human grisaille, a character emerges here and there into somewhat clearer relief because we are better informed about his particular folly or disillusionment.

Flaubert defines the bourgeois as one who 'thinks basely', but he is more accurately defined as one who does not think at all, he 'pursues knowledge'; and since, like Flaubert, he does this 'impersonally' he discovers a reality appropriate to such an attitude—one totally unresponsive to desire or initiative. Balzac, illogically, copies reality *and* protests; and though his protest is neutralized by the implicit content of his novels it at least exists; whereas Flaubert sacrifices it to a widened implicit message.

The implicit is that portion of his statement which the novelist places beyond discussion, beyond the reach of rationalist scepticism; and when, at this level, Flaubert substituted a merciless inhuman 'reality' for Balzac's conventional Christian ethic, he placed severe limitations upon what could be told through identity. To Flaubert's mind this was immaterial since what he was 'telling' was beauty; but except for a few aesthetes and academics Flaubert's appeal is not here; it lies in what he says by default, by virtue of his choosing to express himself in the classical novel which, as we know, is necessarily about identity as a given-proven. Reality, as Flaubert presents it, constitutes an obstacle to the free deployment of identity; so considerable an obstacle in fact that identity will almost always prove to be that of a victim. Flaubert impoverishes identity, and since this is what the classical novel is about, realism from Flaubert onwards will never reach the heights occupied by Balzac. Instead, the novel tends to convey implicitly a 'message' far truer than any to be found implicitly in Balzac; namely, the individual, since he cannot alone change reality, will always be defeated by it. In our society the individual is always alone (since, as we saw, man as praxis—man necessarily *with* his fellows—is a Marxist conception which we refuse to entertain) so that even his material prosperity is a defeat.

Realism after Balzac impoverishes identity, but it certainly does not abolish it; and this results in difficulties and paradoxes for the novel which are worth examining.

Both Lukacs and Goldmann regard *Madame Bovary* and *l'Education Sentimentale* as being novels which confirm their theory of the 'problematic hero'. Let me explain why this seems to me an error.

We have seen how Balzac created the classical novel by concentrating upon a reality (identity) the mere observation of which would constitute in itself a significant moral pronouncement. To say that Flaubert widened the area of the implicit is another way of saying that he extended the 'showing' ('mere observation') to the whole of reality. This is Flaubert's 'impersonality'; he shows a reality which Balzac explicitly denounces. But, as with identity, one can show impersonally only that about which there is general agreement (in the case of identity, bourgeois morality), so that in showing a reality which at every turn betrays man's ideals and desires Flaubert was showing the reality of Malthus, of the 'iron laws of economics', of the 'survival of the fittest'; of those harsh and incontrovertible facts so dear to the nineteenth-century mind which needed above all else a reality for which it would have absolutely no responsibility.

It is of the essence of the problematic, or picaresque hero to interrogate reality. His existence is a question which never receives an answer, and this quest is what the novel is about. In Flaubert, however, there is sufficient an answer for it to be possible to identify the hero; while at the same time that answer is of so 'inhuman' a nature (in contrast to Balzac's traditional morality) that identity cannot 'freely' prove itself. We are confronted in Flaubert (and to a considerable extent in all of subsequent realism) with a subspecies of the classic novel, a novel in which it is *rigorously impossible to determine whether the hero destroys himself or whether he is destroyed by reality.*

In classical fiction to be sure an identity *must* be proven; otherwise we are dealing with some other art form. How then can I talk of an identity which 'freely' proves itself? It is just that, as with Michelangelo's 'prisoners', motionless stone can appear to seethe with muscular strain, so the characters of Balzac and Tolstoy although 'motionless' (possessed of an identity) seem nevertheless to 'choose' the fate that awaits them; largely no doubt because in the worlds of Balzac and Tolstoy alternatives exist, whereas in that of Flaubert they do not. Thus, in *Anna Karenina*, Anna and Vronsky are doomed from the outset, yet the lives of Kitty and Levin suggest that this need not have been. Flaubert rightly discards Tolstoy's anachronistic good and evil, but puts in their place a reality which allows of no choice, which condemns mankind as a whole to defeat and mediocrity. Both Balzac's Lucien de Rubempré and Flaubert's Frédéric Moreau are weak, that is their identity;[9] but there is little reason for Frédéric to attempt to 'prove' anything different. Thus on several occasions Frédéric has the choice of furthering his career or visiting Madame Arnoux; he cannot do both because an ingenious 'reality' has so arranged things that one has to exclude the other (two invitations to dinner on the same evening, etc.). Frédéric always chooses to see Madame Arnoux, and in so doing proves his weakness; but at the same time it is not his fault that circumstances should darkly and patiently align themselves against him. Similarly, Emma Bovary proves herself to be a romantic young woman; but who, given the inhabitants of Yonville-L'Abbaye, could wish to be anything else?

We have seen that the *social* function of the bourgeoisie is *self*-aggrandizement, and that it deals with this contradiction

9 Flaubert calls Frédéric *'l'homme de toutes les faiblesses'* (*l'Education Senti-mentale*, Pléiade, p. 330).

in two ways. On the speculative level it separates value and explanation. Social questions are therefore entirely out of its hands, having been given over to 'specialists' competent to study them objectively. The novelist also observes and studies, but his study is the 'human heart', since reality (except where it is animated with a kind of malevolence as in Flaubert) is properly the concern of science, philosophy, and the various other disciplines. The objective study of reality is an initiative causing the separation of value and explanation to appear part of the nature of things. However, when man himself is observed in this manner the opposite result is produced. We then have a reconciliation of value and explanation which permits the novelist (Balzac and Dickens most conspicuously) to express implicitly an ethos which he explicitly appears to be condemning. He can now resolve social problems into individual ones by asserting that a man's fate is always one he merits—whether we are wealthy or starving, the story of our life is the proof of an identity.

It was remarked a moment ago that Flaubert's total opposition is transformed through his art into total conformism, and we can now see what was meant by that. Flaubert achieves a *complete* separation of value and explanation; a separation which, in a novelist like Balzac, is mitigated by explicit expression. Reality as Flaubert sees it is not a lifeless decor, it is an agent; it may be relied upon to frustrate human desire. From the point of view of nineteenth-century scientism such a notion is absurdly irrational. It is nevertheless (though in a way not intended by Flaubert) profoundly true: not only because people alone—man as identity—are necessarily defeated, but because reality is not a given; it is man himself externalized, a specific cultural project seized into materiality; and in a class society like our own, such materiality is the domination of one class over the others. Flaubert is right, reality is malevolent; but as a result (and we shall return to this in connection with Zola), reality can only be *other men:* '. . . not the gods, not nature but only man himself can be this alien power over man'.[10]

10 Marx, *Economic and Philosophic Manuscripts of 1844*, Lawrence and Wishart, 1959, p. 79.

If philosophy is the history of philosophy then we will look for truth not so much in the conclusions of a particular philosophy as in the intentionality which produced it (the kind of questions which are asked), and this intentionality may well be best revealed in the art of the period which interests us. Flaubert is the artist of positivism. The positivist, like Flaubert, strives to say nothing, and in so doing he maintains a reality which, while not malevolent (this is the greater truth of art), is one in respect to which any expression of value is nonsensical. Such a person (like Flaubert's characters) will be defeated, since his philosophy forbids him to protest effectively against the crimes and stupidities of a government acting in his name; furthermore the defeat (again as in Flaubert's novels) will, contradictorily, have been chosen; it will be the proof of an identity, the expression of cultural distinction, of a rich private realm suspended knowingly above the petty passions of the time. The reality of positivism is one against which we are powerless, and this is essential if man is to be entity rather than, as in Marx and Sartre, project. In *Les Mots* Sartre speaks of the 'abstract hatred' of man implicit in nineteenth-century aestheticism. In *l'Education Sentimentale*, for example, we find this: '. . . there are situations in which the least cruel of men is so detached from others that he could, quite unmoved, watch the whole human race perish.'[11] Or again, Frédéric, finding himself in one of the embattled streets of Paris in 1848: '. . . had the impression of being at a show'.[12] For western scientism the world is a spectacle, and whether we are looking for beauty, the 'deferred meaning' of positivism, or the absurd of contemporary intellectuals, what we are really watching are the various genocides —accomplished, in progress, or merely planned—which form part of the civilizing mission of the west.

ZOLA

In trying to avoid the necessity of 'telling' in the novel Flaubert implicitly tells of his class and culture with a plenitude perhaps unequalled in the history of classical fiction. In his novelette

11 Pléiade, p. 315.
12 *Ibid.*, p. 318.

Un Coeur Simple, however something has changed, and trying to decide exactly what it is will serve as an excellent introduction to Zola.

We have argued that the whole problem of the nineteenth-century novel was to discover a reality the mere description of which would constitute in itself a statement. But if identity is to be that reality, then the pertinence of the statement will be increasingly compromised as industry and its cities bring into being masses of people who dumbly and passively endure processes against which they are almost defenceless; or, when in desperation they fight back, what they accomplish will be a function of their *degree of solidarity*, of the success they have in *not* breaking down into individuals. In brief, the novel was in danger of becoming more and more obviously the expression of a class and so entering into contradiction with the rationalist claim of universality.

It is as though Flaubert were aware of this; hence his attempt to transform the explicit into beauty so that the novel could show not only identity, but a reality independent of it. As it turned out, however, the choice did not exist; for reality, as in Balzac, must yield to whatever the successful demonstration of an identity may require. The balance may then be at least partially redressed on the explicit level; whereas if reality is treated in itself, identity can no longer be deployed with the same freedom and the novel as a form is diminished in proportion.

Suppose now that the novelist accepts the impoverishment just mentioned, might not this loss (a small one in appearance since identity rests upon the idiocy of bourgeois morality) be compensated for by showing a victim who is far better than what destroys him? In other words, might not what the novel tells consist in showing that the good can be persecuted because they are good and not as a result of their identity having been mistaken? By 'good' will be meant not good in the narrow sense of what is generally approved of, but good as the reverse of everything the bourgeois does (as opposed to what he says he does); good, in other words, as complete self-forgetfulness through devotion to others. If, furthermore, it is made clear that such a person is not being persecuted by the implacable 'personified' reality of *Madame Bovary,* and *l'Education Senti-*

mentale (and of the work of a Maupassant, or a Hardy, and many others down even to Robbe-Grillet in *Les Gommes*) but by a society defectively organized, will it not be practicable at last to reconcile showing and telling without having to submit to the narrowness of vision and the partiality imposed by identity?

On however small a scale this is what Flaubert attempts in *Un Coeur Simple*. He asks what kind of a society it is in which a woman like Félicité who lives in and for others should never have known human companionship and is reduced finally to that of a parrot. Félicité, like Dostoevsky's Myshkin, is regarded condescendingly as a fool because she realizes the highest moral aspirations of her culture. The achievement of *Un Coeur Simple* (and, later, of Zola's two greatest novels, *l'Assommoir* and *Germinal*) is that something of great importance should have been said purely and simply by showing, without the novelist offering a single interpretation, suggestion, or aside. When Balzac intervenes explicitly he ceases momentarily to work on a novel, but without his novel becoming a political pamphlet or a moral treatise. He does this so often one wonders how his fiction could have survived such treatment and, inversely, why Flaubert (*Un Coeur Simple*) and Zola should not have achieved a solution to the problem of the classical novel.

We know the answer—one cannot hedge in identity without cramping the novel itself. But let me phrase it differently: the classical novel will not tolerate that uncertainty which is of the essence of the picaresque. If the novelist seeks to protest (as in an alienated society he must) then he is obliged to do so explicitly (with the consequences we have indicated) otherwise we no longer know what the novel is about. Let us look at *l'Assommoir*.

Zola's Gervaise in this novel may be compared to Flaubert's Félicité in that she comes to grief because of her fine qualities, while the Lorilleux succeed because they possess those virtues our society always rewards: selfishness, blind industry, high 'moral standards', contempt or hatred for one's fellows. Zola tells us all this in the most effective way possible, by simply showing it. But how can the terrible things which are related here happen? Because Gervaise is the kind of woman she is, or because her society is such as it is? (It will be recalled that with Balzac's Lucien de Rubempré there was no difficulty; Lucien's fate is the proof of his identity, while social reality is either simply a function of identity or is dealt with explicitly.) We are not at all sure exactly what is being shown and, thereby, said. The result is not the rich ambiguity of the best picaresque (*Don Quixote, The Castle*) but a sort of blurring.[13]

The classical novel shows its characters 'freely' proving themselves to be what they already were. Zola's purpose was to show the social order as the determining factor in what happens to people; to show that poverty was not, as the bourgeoisie liked to think, the inevitable consequence of a particular identity. Hence Zola intended *l'Assommoir* to be: '. . . a horrifying tableau which would point its own moral';[14] and of Gervaise he says: '. . . her misfortunes were not of her own doing'.[15] Her husband, a roof worker, unaccountably has a fall, and his injuries induce in him a dread of his work which is the beginning of the end for his family. Copeau's

---

13 If we consider, as I suggest, Stendhal and Dostoevsky to be in important respects 'contemporary novelists', then Tolstoy is undoubtedly the greatest novelist of the classical period, and we can readily see why: he maintains the two levels of discourse but, in a supreme formal achievement, renders them all but indistinguishable. Or, to express this differently, Tolstoy's protest *takes the form of identity*, and this was possible (to mention only one factor) because of his conversion to a form of Christianity which was considerably less an instrument of class rule than that prevalent in the France of Balzac. *The Death of Ivan Ilyich* is as scathing a denunciation of middle-class values as is to be found anywhere, yet Tolstoy is in appearance concerned exclusively with the character of his hero; so that, as in Balzac, the two levels of discourse exist and are in direct contradiction since identity, far from enabling us to combat middle-class values, is the very foundation upon which they rest.

I do not think, incidentally, that one can talk of a change of identity in this novel, the whole point being that Ivan had been dead all his life and is 'born' only at death's door. We have, all of us, for Tolstoy, a common humanity in Christ which gets 'hidden' by the worldly requirements of modern society. Death returns to Ivan his humanity. The 'message' of Tolstoy is the exact reverse of that of Flaubert: for Tolstoy, salvation is an ever present possibility, for Flaubert we must reconcile ourselves to a progressive disillusionment. Both are wrong, as we know, since in common with the entire nineteenth century, they insisted upon posing problems of concern to the collectivity in terms of individuals—the consequence, as we have seen, of our determination to retain individual ownership despite the 'socialization' of labour.

14 *l'Assommoir*, Pléiade, p. 1543.

15 *Ibid.*, p. 648.

fall is not an identity in process of demonstration, but an example of the terrible precariousness of working-class existence. But even if we grant that Copeau's fall from the roof was something that happened *to* him, entirely apart from any responsibility of his, it is impossible to take the same attitude toward his refusal to return to regular work; so that we have a recurrence of the problem Flaubert faced; even by personifying reality he was unable to keep us from seeing that Frédéric Moreau was his own worst enemy.

Zola's answer to this problem was to place the reality he wished to condemn *within* his characters in the form of an alcoholism which he supposed could be hereditary; so that when we read: "She [Gervaise] knew herself, she hadn't a penny's worth of will power",[16] we are perhaps intended to understand that Gervaise's lack of will is an identity 'passed on to her', one imposed by a corrupt and unjust social order. If this were possible, however, novel writing could not exist since there would be *only* reality which is absurd because the real cannot copy itself; it has to be 'constituted' by an initiative which *is* man, as Gervaise *is* the act by which she knows herself, and not some known entity. One cannot suppress freedom without suppressing what human life is in its essence, and we should expect to find Zola referring to: '. . . the damnable existence she [Gervaise] had made for herself'.[17] But this is not what he wanted to say either, nor is it altogether true.

Zola no doubt represents the most conscientious attempt made by a nineteenth-century novelist to turn his art against the class which produced it; but this is clearly not practicable. He was understood exactly in so far as he had capitulated. If Gervaise was the innocent victim of an inhuman environment, so are we all—the factory owner was the first to deplore the 'iron laws' of the economy. If, on the contrary, Gervaise was free, then she had brought her fate upon herself, and the well-fed reader remains as guiltless as before.

We can see then that the highest achievement in classical fiction is inseparable from a characterization which is at every moment, and inextricably, determined and free (given-proven),

16 *Ibid.*, p. 705.
17 *Ibid.*, p. 796.

which is to say that the determinism must be 'moral' rather than 'scientific' in nature. The novel could not afford to be too intelligent, hence the strong political conservatism which marked all the great classical novelists. One need only compare a novel like *Sister Carrie* with a far greater book like *Anna Karenina* to see that the novelist was not free to despise middle-class morality. Dreiser points out, among other things, that a girl may be wiser to live comfortably and usefully as someone's mistress than to survive wretchedly as an honest working girl. But Dreiser's truth and common sense leave Carrie relatively 'characterless' (that is, without a moral beyond) and this is not the way to greatness in the novel. What is required is a heroine like Anna Karenina who learns that the wages of sin are death; or a couple like Kitty and Levin, in the same novel, who shun the corruptions of high society and instead pursue the simple but enduring pleasures of life on the farm.

As soon as the novelist accepts that it should be his business to show, he concedes everything; for if what he shows is to be intelligible it can only be with reference to something beyond.[18] It is what we call mind that makes this liaison, and success will clearly depend upon how totally it is divorced from preoccupations which are those of any particular group. The 'watcher at the window' may have his sympathies, he may even indicate them, but he must on no account *participate*. These considerations are important to a reading of Zola's *Germinal*, in which he seems to have tried to overcome the difficulties mentioned in connection with *l'Assommoir* by showing the poor less as individuals (and therefore as 'always being with us' since, whether determined or free, they are no one's responsibility) than as members of a collectivity.

In theory much was to be gained in this way since the reader could be immersed in an entire isolated mining community and thus made to see that these people were not individuals, but products of the mine. Gervaise, thanks to her shop, might have 'bettered herself'; for the miners, there was simply no way out, and in fact even to think in such

18 The other two possibilities are that what is shown is absurd, or that there is nothing to show because there is no given. But the classical novel is one which by definition could not entertain these alternatives.

terms could easily be felt as a betrayal of one's comrades. But if there was no freedom for the poor as a community, there was no determinism either, because when the miners organized to strike they took a step towards becoming the subjects rather than the objects of history.

To use an expression like the 'subjects of history', however, and to intend it literally, is to leave the confines not only of bourgeois rationalism but of all pre-Marxist thought which never saw itself as an aspect of a given praxis, but always as the finally successful Answer which had for one reason or another escaped the philosophers of the past. The achievement of positivism was to point out that the error of philosophers had been to philosophize, and even today the English-speaking philosopher regards with bewildered amusement the persistence of this anachronistic activity on the continent. Zola, like Flaubert, was a victim of the superstition of the disembodied eye, of this non-doctrine which of all doctrines has been, at least for the past thirty or forty years, the most hypocritically obtuse.

In practising the art of the novel Zola participated; and since the classical novel can tell only by showing, Zola, despite himself, participated on the wrong side. To show with maximum fidelity meant, for the nineteenth-century, to remove oneself to a vantage point above partisan feeling from which the 'whole' would be visible. But this of course is precisely the separation of value and explanation peculiar to bourgeois rationalism; and what Zola took to be his impartiality was in reality an *act* by which he condemned as an error, however understandable a one, the miners' 'partial', passionate reaction to circumstances. A careful enough reading of the last page or two of *Germinal* shows Zola, perhaps reluctantly, coming down on the side of order and suggesting that, in the ripeness of time, conditions would improve.

In view of what the reader learns of life in the mines and in the homes of the miners, there is an involuntary cynicism in such a conclusion that Zola could have avoided only by understanding that there was no reality to show. There were two conflicting praxes (Marx's class struggle) one of which (that of the bourgeoisie) consisted, in part, in alleging that there exists an intelligible Real in addition to the products of

93

human activities. If this criterion is adopted we can see that practically all Marxist thought failed to disengage itself from a world view which Marx had rendered obsolete. To postulate the existence of 'laws of history', 'dialectical' or not, is to establish a beyond thanks to which the stultifying business of 'identifying' men can be continued, this time on a class rather than an individual basis. Zola as a novelist, consequently, would have gained nothing by committing himself to the Marxism of his day; on the contrary he might have been led to cretinize his art by seeing in the miners people who were, simply by virtue of being workers (that is, instruments of the laws of history), 'better' than representatives of all other social classes.

There was a sound basis upon which Zola could have preferred the poor and fought for them but it is difficult to see how he could have done so through the novel as it then existed. For if man is praxis, then there is nothing to show except his 'products', and the essential escapes. There is nothing to tell either, except the success or failure of a collective enterprise; and whether it be one or the other there is no moral involved, but only a greater or lesser accuracy in evaluating all the relevant factors.

It was said a moment ago that the miners were 'products of the mine'. But how can men (an orientated activity) be a product of the mine (a thing). This could only be so if the mine (and the economy as a whole) *were* the bourgeoisie itself, and if we are faithful to our premises, this is the conclusion we must draw; for if man is praxis, then he is no thing; but then there can be nothing 'between' him and his products, he *is* his products.[19]

---

19 The philosophical 'contradictions' which can be pointed out in the work of Marx could not have been avoided *at that time;* for Marx had both to talk a language which would be comprehensible to his contemporaries (hence his scientism) and, if he were to be a truly revolutionary thinker, abandon classical rationalism (hence his 'illogical' indignations, his structuralism, etc.). With scientism disposed of, the contemporary Marxist no longer faces this dilemma, and if we look back at Marx from Sartre the 'contradictions' disappear. When, for example, Marx says that man is the product of his labour, we can take this literally only if we understand Sartre's *Being and Nothingness* in which man: 'is what he is not, and is not what he is'. Man *is* his products since, in addition, there is no thing, no

Identity, however, exists precisely to enable us to elude such a conclusion. The bourgeois maintains that he is something in addition to what he owns, that his property is the confirmation of an identity and that, inversely, the indigence of the worker indicates a person of an inferior kind. This provides us with that sound basis for a choice mentioned a moment ago, for the bourgeoisie *acts with the intention of being able to deny that it does so*; that is to say, it expropriates the products of its society which then become the sign or proof of an inner endowment which is thing, not praxis. This is why the worker, for Marx, represented the hope of mankind. The worker, having nothing, *was* nothing; nothing that is except his labour, except that praxis which man *is*. The whole middle-class way of life, however, is geared to the vital necessity of proving that we are not 'just men'; we are first of all doctors, authors, successful business men and so forth. Similarly, women are not fellow creatures, our collaborators in a social praxis, but creatures of a specific kind; they are sexual objects, they are 'irrational', bereft of creative gifts, they are everything which is 'typically feminine'.

We have seen how recourse to mistaken identity enabled the nineteenth-century novelist to imagine he was dealing with social abuses. A reader who in real life would have been appalled to find himself in the company of a thief, prostitute or factory worker might become sentimental over a fictionalized account of the lives of such people because the novel would explain how they were not really what they appeared to be. But this of course is bourgeois 'universalism' at its most stupidly naïve, and the more cultivated public was not closed to the notion of the relativity of moral values; in other words, what if the character is part of a group whose beyond is not ours? How is he to be identified? This I think was the fascination of Mérimée's Carmen in respect to whom the

---

entity (man is consciousness which is intentionality); and yet at the same time he 'is not what he is', since if there were only thing, there could be no creative labour. When men work to rule they supply labour as a thing, but withhold what Marx called their 'labour power'; in other words that free 'intentional' activity which man is, and which creates surplus value— the wealth of certain social groups which we prefer to consider the 'wealth of nations'.

reader is obliged to suspend judgment, for he can judge neither as a Spanish gypsy nor as himself since he belongs to a culture whose morality Carmen rejects and despises. Presumably, therefore, Mérimée was 'telling' of the relativity of moral values by 'showing' Carmen, for we are unable to determine the kind of person she is. But if the universalization of bourgeois moral values is stupid, the universalization of one's point of view is impossible. Carmen exists necessarily *for us*. She is, for example, promiscuous; and while we can 'make allowances', we cannot see her in any other light. So that Carmen is judged, but the judgment is then mitigated by the understanding that she is not one of us.

When the strike of the miners of *Germinal* turns to rioting Zola expects the reader, in view of the terrible conditions in which the miners lived and worked, to suspend judgment. But this is not possible. The miners ceased to be individuals to become a destructive mob, and understanding how the miners could have been brought to such a pass simply enabled the 'enlightened' bourgeoisie to imagine it had placed itself above class interest. An Englishman can understand the Frenchman's anger or irritation at being addressed by a stranger as *tu* instead of *vous*, but he can never experience it. So the understanding of the bourgeois intellectual never touches the *experience* of poverty and violence, it is closed up within a different praxis, *and it is an instrument of that praxis*. This is why it is naïve to suppose the liberal or socialist could 'betray'; his enlightened objectivity serves only to perpetuate the myth of a reality which is given, of which we can therefore pursue knowledge in view of a better understanding. But as we have seen, that reality *is* the dominant social class.

The bourgeois defends his property as his life because it *is* his life; the complexity of an individual is the complexity of that part of the social product (cultural as well as material) he has been able to make his own. His complexity is exterior to him. For Zola's readers, on the contrary, present as well as past, that complexity is a man's 'inner world' (the subject matter of novelists like Joyce or James), it is his individuality. When consequently the miners turn to violence they cease to be individuals, they become a mob, they temporarily lose the use of their reason, they fall into animality. It is now safe to 'make allowances'; for in so far as the worker remains an individual he is defeated by the social and economic apparatus which *is* the bourgeoisie, and in so far as he does not, he ceases to be fully and completely a man, he ceases to be one of us.

Toward the end of *Critique de la Raison Dialectique,* Sartre explains how the nineteenth-century industrialist could compete with other rugged individuals and yet form with them a group capable of forwarding with great efficiency certain collective purposes. Yet whenever this 'we' in which every 'I' necessarily inheres emerges to dissolve the materiality which condemns us all to frustration and solitude we are frightened by the spectacle of individuals 'losing their identity in the group',[20] as though individualism were any more than the 'freedom' to devote ourselves exclusively to demonstrating an identity while the public realm becomes simply a means by which the semi-literate and power-hungry can do the same.

The miners of *Germinal* consequently did not 'degenerate into a mob' except from *our* point of view, and to accept theirs would have meant acceding to what Sartre calls "another world";[21] one in which the subject is collective, one therefore to which the classical novel is quite foreign.

By the time we reach *La Condition Humaine* the 'mob' of *Germinal* has become a fighting unit whose right to 'destroy' no one would think of contesting. And yet Malraux's novel is about the impossibility of communicating with one's fellows—a 'problem' which could not conceivably exist for the collective subject of a revolutionary movement. It is only within the

20 Whether of left or right, intellectuals share this dread which enables them to consider communism and fascism as cut from much the same cloth. So that, according to Eric Fromm, fascism indicates a longing in modern man 'to forget his self as a separate entity' and to find a 'new and fragile security at the expense of sacrificing the integrity of his individual self' (*The Fear of Freedom,* p. 221). This is nonsense. Fascism is bourgeois democracy grown militant in the face of communism; it is middle-class terror of falling into the anonymity of the masses. To avoid this it is determined at any cost to preserve the material apparatus which is its respectability, its 'distinction', its individualism. Communism exists to destroy that apparatus, so that the communist *is* in so far as he contributes to the task, in so far as he does; he has no 'individual self' to 'sacrifice' (he is usually a starving peasant) and the measure in which he might acquire one would be the extent of his betrayal.

21 *Critique de la Raison Dialectique,* p. 645.

bourgeois planetarium of majestically orbiting egos that the need is felt for some system of communication, something like gravitation which will assign the lesser to the weightier bodies and keep us all whirling around God. The passing of this scheme of things has not given us a wish for 'another world'; instead our thought degenerates into nostalgic claptrap or we are petrified by the absurdity of it all.

STENDHAL

Stendhal does not belong in a book about the classical novel, for he is the first contemporary novelist. I want nevertheless to discuss him as briefly as possible so as to show that it is from the standpoint of the hypothesis I am suggesting that we can best appreciate exactly what Stendhal did to the novel to be so astonishingly in advance of his time.

We have seen that, throughout its history, from Cervantes to the present, the exercise of reason in the form of scepticism is inseparable from the novel. In classical fiction, however, the scepticism becomes 'explicit', it becomes peripheral so that the reader can, if he wishes, eliminate it to the advantage of an implicit statement often in direct contradiction with the explicit. But not only is this implicit content (identity as a given-proven) absent in Stendhal, his work cannot be fully understood except as the *exposure of identity as a colossal confidence trick*. To see this clearly, however, we shall have to consider in what ways the contemporary and historical picaresque differ from one another.

Both question and contest, but each does so with reference to radically different criteria. The historical picaresque calls society to account in the name of reason and common sense; and if the hero roams over considerable distances encountering people from every trade and walk of life it is so that the author can demonstrate the universal validity of reason. This does not mean he offered solutions (although some, like Richardson and Rousseau, might make the attempt) but the general feeling was that solutions existed if only men would be patient and above all removed their allegiance from the tragi-comic practices and superstitions surviving from the 'dark ages'. (Anglo-Saxon philosophy is still at this point: the answers exist if only thinkers would refrain from metaphysics.) If the modern picaresque also contests then it must contest the very regime the historical helped bring into being; and if this contestation is to be radical (as it undoubtedly is) it will not be able—any more than Marx was able—to utilize reason as traditionally understood in our culture. Upon what grounds then did Stendhal mount an attack against his society so telling that his contemporaries (and many present-day readers as well) were obliged not to understand him? They understood Balzac well enough because he reasoned with them and because however damning he might become explicitly there was always the rest of the novel, the novel proper, the story about a reality which was their reality, society viewed from their particular and peculiar vantage point. The more shockingly conclusive the reasoning of a Vautrin might become, the more obviously it was the product of a 'diseased mind', of an identity demonstrating itself in this way.

We have seen that the great difficulty of bourgeois culture has been to attribute a *public* significance to a life of *private* aggrandizement; and this it does in part by contending that acts which appear to be inspired by mere vulgar acquisitiveness are on the contrary determined by reality and/or constitute a proof of identity. But if there is no genuine human initiative, how is it that all we are immediately and indubitably aware of is precisely such initiative; a relentless, life-long effort (of which the life of Balzac—but not that of Stendhal—is a notable example) to enrich or at least to 'better' ourselves. Fortunately such awareness is 'subjective' and hence one can simply deny it exists; or, in company where this might provoke laughter, there is always reason, with the help of which it can be demonstrated first that the facts being such I had no alternative,[22] and second, my intentions are very different from

22 One of the most important factors contributing to the liberalization of life in the west since Victorian times (the relaxation of attitudes toward dress, sex, raising of children, etc.) is the increasing plausibility of this alibi. The modern shareholder is less directly responsible for the conduct of his industry than was the nineteenth-century entrepreneur; and, more generally, the entire 'materiality' of life has grown to such proportions that we can pose more successfully as its 'victims'. There is less distance between what we do (since we are 'helpless') and what we profess, and it was this distance which led the nineteenth-century bourgeoisie to impose upon itself those preposterous constraints which were intended to demonstrate that man is not initiative but thing.

those which the practical results of what I do might lead you to infer. Reason, in the traditional sense, can only be exercised upon what is; but since what is is in reality never given, but constituted in the light of a more or less conscious collective project, reason ceases to be primordial and becomes an aspect of a praxis for which it is vital that reality be regarded as a given. To be reasonable is to be resigned; and Zola, despite himself, is obliged to consider that his miners were 'unreasonable'.

Stendhal never deigns to reason, to argue, or to explain; he simply states and if you are unable to see what he means it is because you prefer not to, so there is no point in insisting. There is no longer any question of knowing or not knowing, being right or wrong, good or bad; the real issue is: *how much of what you are irrefutably aware are you prepared to acknowledge?*

There are consequently no characters in the classical sense in Stendhal's novels. There are rather people who have made one of two fundamental choices in life; the first consists in adjusting word and deed to the requirements of whatever self we have selected of those proposed by our society; the second is simply the refusal to have any part in so contemptible a comedy.[23]

Stendhal's heroes are not people of a certain kind, they are simply 'what is left' when the frippery and the genuflecting is put aside. They are the child-like anonymity which precedes the assumption of a 'responsible' role in life.[24] Whatever their social origin (Fabrice del Dongo is an aristocrat, Lucien Leuwen a bourgeois, Lamiel and Julien Sorel are not far from the bottom) they are strangers to their fellows for refusing the identity assigned to them, for refusing to act in a predictable manner except in so far as they act hypocritically so as to maintain some contact, however fragile, with others. Julien Sorel is described as being 'oblivious to himself',[25] and this is Stendhal's *one* criterion. The value of a man or woman is

23 Contemptible because people cleave to an approved self largely through fear, that fear of ridicule which Stendhal refers to so often as dominating the lives of the elegant and refined who are, in Valéry's words, 'devoured by others'. The happy free individual of our society is terrified of his neighbour who is always a *judge*.

24 Sartre describes this sad process in *l'Enfance d'un Chef*.

25 *Jamais de retour sur lui-même, Le Rouge et le Noir*, Garnier, 1958, p. 291.

always in direct proportion to the degree of spontaneity of which they are capable. We are obliged, for instance, to temper somewhat our liking for Mathilde de La Mole because of the histrionic element she introduces into her love for Julien, while Madame de Rênal's deplorably primitive religion is no impediment to the admiration her superb 'simplicity' excites in us. Madame Grandet (*Lucien Leuwen*) is saved when, having fallen in love, she forgets she is a *Grande Dame*. We can have sympathy for the Marquis de La Mole because he is prepared to admit that his whole way of life belongs to another age, and that he is best employed in tending to his pleasures.

Stendhal's view of men and of his time comes to wonderfully concise expression in Julien Sorel's incredulity as he watches the bishop of Agde practise giving his blessing in front of a mirror. Julien's wordless amazement is the only argument he uses against his enemies, since you cannot enlighten people who know as well as you do that their life is one long attempt *to produce the desired effect*. They must know this since they are obliged to practise the appropriate words and gestures which they then put forward as proof of a given self.

We remember Stendhal's characters not for what they are, but for what they do. They are only in so far as they do; they are, a century before existentialism, the 'sum of their acts'. The extreme susceptibility of the heroes of Stendhal is that of people with no self-esteem to fall back upon. Their entire being is at stake at every moment, so that Lucien Leuwen is tormented for weeks by the memory of an insult he had failed to avenge. Narrative in Stendhal serves to construct, not to reveal a character. Sanseverina's various 'immoralities', far from enabling us to detect some hidden corruption, prove her capable of despising those life-destroying conventions to which the mediocre adhere by way of soliciting a favourable judgment as to who they are.

Identity is a nucleus around which the 'inner world' is organized; eliminate the former and the latter should go as well.[26] So it is in Stendhal. We know Mosca is jealous because

26 Otherwise (as with Flaubert's exterior reality bereft of the moral law) the novelist shows with nothing to tell unless, as did Flaubert, he calls upon formal values to make good the deficiency. But aestheticism in the novel, as we saw in the case of Flaubert, is a device enabling the cultivated

on one occasion he clutches at his dagger; this movement *is* his jealousy which is therefore a comportment and not an 'inner state'. The love of Madame de Rênal for Julien has no existence 'in itself', we are told only of what she *does*; she has dresses sent from Paris for the first time in her life, she takes many foolhardy risks and, finally, dies a few days after Julien's execution. All we know of Valenod in the same novel is that he appropriates funds intended for the poor. If, in the best humanist tradition, we attempted to understand Valenod, we would discover that 'inside' he was not all that bad. But Stendhal, obstinately, can see no further than what Valenod actually does. (So that, if Stendhal were alive today, he would have seen in Johnson, Rusk, Rostow and company, a band of moronic murderers, whereas we know they were responsible statesmen, moved by the best intentions, doing what could be done in a very difficult situation.)

Omniscience in fiction, as we have seen, creates the world it proposes to reveal. It creates a spectator's world, one in which correct observance of both ourselves and of others will enable us to adjust our conduct to the identities involved. There is also a spectator's battle of Waterloo: a battle the 'causes' of which we can pursue knowledge; there is the battle which is one of the

---

man of letters to remain at one with his class without appearing to do so; without showing a world as carefully narrowed as that of a Thackeray or a Trollope or as morally simple-minded as that of Dickens. Thus Flaubert does not hesitate to show us the troubles of 1848; we listen to the orators, watch the fighting, and are forced to the conclusion that, with one side as contemptible as the other, no choice is possible. Similarly, in *The Princess Casamassima* we are free to hobnob with anarchists, to discover even that they are decent chaps on the whole; but once again, no choice is possible. The hero, Hyacinth, commits suicide unable to decide between revolt and our 'heritage of culture'. For Flaubert we are powerless against a malignant reality, for James nothing must take precedence over that culture which feeds the inner realm. In each case the conclusion is incontrovertible because we have 'understood the other fellow's point of view', we have 'seen both sides of the question'. We sympathize with Daisy Miller's revolt against convention, but on condition she remain chaste. All James is there: he sympathizes with the London poor, but on condition they prefer culture to bread. Sartre has said that one human life weighs more for him than the cathedral of Chartres. When the battle lines are drawn James and his like will always be found (by default perhaps, but inevitably) on the side of the cathedral against any number of human lives. No regime ever received support more valuable than the phony opposition of the objective aestheticizing intellectual.

great moments of an heroic people, an everlasting example; there is the Waterloo of the scale models in the war museums, not very different from that of the statesmen and the high-ranking none of whom were buried on the field, nor very different either from that of the classical novelist writing usually in the spirit of the phrase with which Balzac often introduces his historical and descriptive passages: 'This will require an explanation.' The ensuing explanation, however, will take us very far from the event as lived or experienced by each individual participant; and if we insist upon recounting this alone, then we seize reality; but then also we discover reality to be 'absurd'. Fabrice del Dongo's experience of the Battle of Waterloo had in it the seeds of Roquentin's experience of the objects around him in Sartre's *La Nausée*. In each case we discover there to be no common measure between what we subjectively apprehend, and what a given collectivity decrees to be real. Waterloo for Fabrice is the world gone mad; riderless horses, incoherent men, scattered explosions and skirmishes, disfigured corpses . . .; just as objects, for Roquentin, are what Sartre would eventually call *en-soi*, the 'stuff' of which praxis creates an 'arbitrarily' meaningful world. To recount the Battle of Waterloo 'objectively' is not to discover intelligibility where Fabrice found only chaos; it is to construct a world where there exists a meaning independent of human praxis; it is to take an initiative the nature of which as a matter of principle remains unexamined. Imagine the death of a father who was not particularly admired or liked by his children. They have gathered for a day to divide a small inheritance. There is much good-humoured reminiscing, perhaps even a little merry-making. This event would have been absolutely without significance for those present, while the same incident related in a classical novel would *necessarily* have had a meaning; it would have been, perhaps, a commentary on 'human callousness'. History as usually written is the 'novel of mankind', and whether meaning is explicit (Spengler, Toynbee) or implicit (academic donkey work) it must exist, otherwise it is exceedingly difficult to see the point of it all.

Stendhal's achievement is that he both rejects the existence of objective meaning and does so on the only grounds which could make that rejection definitive: on grounds of subjective evidence, of what we all know except in so far as we succeed in reasoning it away. Hence religion does not exist for Stendhal, not because he has 'sound reasons' for not believing in God, but because he is unable to do so without a deliberate effort. On the basis of this 'personal peculiarity' Stendhal concludes that religion in his society was, in general, something people were *doing* for transparent reasons. Flaubert had no religious belief either, but his atheism was that of all nineteenth-century humanism: the lay theology of scientism, that weird religion in which man contemplates not God but his Works; a religion whose moral exigencies may be fully satisfied by expressing the pious wish that man might come first; when he does not, then it is the fault of 'reality', never of what some people do.

Only in the most superficial respects (his love of landscape, for example) does Stendhal bear any resemblance to other novelists of the century, and when readers fail to be struck by this it is because they are reluctant to associate revolutionary content with orthodox form. But, as we have seen, form in the novel *is* content; so that the strictly formal differences between Balzac and Kafka are negligible compared to those between Delacroix and Cézanne, Hugo and Mallarmé, etc. The hero of Camus's *l'Etranger* is destroyed by his society because he refuses to provide himself with that 'human nature' which enables us to obey 'freely' the dictates of our particular group or culture. Meursault describes himself as being 'exactly like everyone else'. This is true; the only difference is that he will not feign those thoughts or feelings alleged to belong to a 'normal man', those appropriate reactions we all heartily provide as our guarantee of a correct identity. This is precisely the story of Julien Sorel, even down to the pistol shots and the trial. A century and a half before Salinger in *The Catcher in the Rye* discovered with a sense of outrage the universal phoniness of our society, Stendhal had said what could be said, and without, like Salinger, proceeding to besot himself with mysticism. The court of Parma in *La Chartreuse de Parme* is exactly contemporary America trying to pretend that the Russian and Chinese Revolutions did not take place, just as Stendhal's contemporaries tried to persuade themselves that the French Revolution was an historical accident.

The paradox of Stendhal is that he should have expressed notions of such precocity *as though they went absolutely without saying.*[27] Since he was not regarded as mad, his contemporaries must have understood him. In other words, the perspective Stendhal had upon his society was the result not of his taking up a new philosophy which the men of his time would have had difficulty in understanding; on the contrary, it followed from his realization that we are fully equipped to survive on this earth (this was the great lesson of the French Revolution, that the social order is made and not decreed) and when we fail it is not for having fallen short of the truth, but for refusing to acknowledge truths incompatible with our privileges or prejudices.

Stendhal is the first modern man. In his work that 'definitive victory' over the gods which Gide hopes for in his *Thésée* is already accomplished. The 'hidden god' of science and of morality is gone, and along with him the possibility of that implicit discourse in fiction which enabled the classical novelist to support a regime he appeared to be denouncing.

---

27 It does not seem to me that Lukacs's theory of the 'problematic hero' can be applied very successfully to Stendhal whose significance lies precisely in the fact that he makes the picaresque search for meaning obsolete. Stendhal never forgot that 'other world' which he entered, still almost a child, when he accompanied the French revolutionary troops into Italy. This is what must be borne constantly in mind in thinking about Stendhal—that he was a revolutionary (taking the word 'revolutionary' in the sense of 'pure praxis', not in the sense of idea) surviving into a period of restoration. In other words, the hero of Stendhal is a member of a revolutionary collectivity (for which there is no truth or error in the absolute, but only the more or less successful response to concrete situations) trying to live after that collectivity had given place to an individualism seeking truth (pursuing knowledge) as a means of self-identification, as a means of concealing a praxis of discrimination and oppression. The difficulty of life, for Stendhal, arises not from the limitations of man's intelligence, ingenuity, good-will and so forth, but from his hypocrisy; in other words, from the limitations of his *courage.* (All of contemporary thought—Husserl, Freud, Sartre—was to take this direction: the difficulty is not to know, but to elucidate what is already known, so that virtue or vice become authenticity or bad faith.)

5 The case of Dickens

It is in the novel that the bourgeoisie expresses most completely its vision of things, and if the novel is about identity as a given-proven, then bourgeois art reaches its 'highest' and purest form in soap opera and the detective story.

We prefer of course to look upon mass entertainment as an embarrassing excrescence produced by the incurable stupidity of the average man upon the otherwise sound body of our culture. But apart from the concept of identity bourgeois culture does not exist: it is made up, on the one hand, of what we have been able to salvage from past cultures (hence the importance of history for us) and, on the other, of our attempts, through what is best in contemporary art and thought since the turn of the century, to see and think outside the framework of bourgeois rationalism.

The novel is that extraordinary art form which degenerates in proportion as what it is about emerges more clearly; so that no sooner had Balzac discovered in identity the means of creating the classical novel than he was obliged to occupy the reader's attention with other things, chiefly with a keenly perceptive explicit commentary upon middle-class government and values. The best classical novelists, in other words, were aware that what could be told by showing identity would have to be supplemented by somehow telling, in addition, that certain ancient values would have to be more strictly observed if all ties between the individual and the public realm were not to be severed and society handed over to the irresponsible rapacity of the dealers in money. Hence Balzac's 'throne and altar', Tolstoy's revivalism, Faulkner's frontier. Balzac and Tolstoy, however, lived in countries still largely pre-industrial; and when the novel is obliged (if it is to continue to show) to confront the misery of the newly urbanized poor the result is the impoverishment of identity (and consequently of the novel itself) to the advantage of a reality which, since it is not the 'externalization of man' (as in Marx) can only be dealt with 'objectively'; that is, ineffectually.

106

Dickens lived in the 'workshop of the world' and at a time when its economic power (which began to decline well before 1914) had about reached its peak. And yet Dickens felt obliged neither (like Balzac and Tolstoy) to plead for a return to what was taken to be the greater social responsibility of previous ages, nor (like Zola) to show reality as honestly as he knew how.[1] If bourgeois art comes to magnificent untrammelled flower in the television serials it is because the poor have been reduced to numbers which can be safely ignored, and because starvation has been pushed outside our national boundaries. In the bourgeois mind no problem resists the proliferation of goods; so that both explicit indignation and the impoverishment of identity in realism have become superfluous. But this may be said also of Dickens who lived well before the blessed generalization of affluence[2], and this makes him of all the classical novelists the most flagrantly and unrepentantly middle class. But then how will we account for Dickens's undoubted superiority over a novelist like Victor Hugo who shows so much more genuine sympathy and understanding for the unfortunate? We have already encountered a similar problem in comparing Tolstoy and Dreiser and the answer is the same: the novel more easily

1 As Orwell points out in his essay on Dickens, there is not a single representative of the working class in all Dickens's novels with the exception of Stephen Blackpool in *Hard Times* who, incidentally, refuses to support his fellow workers in a strike, thereby qualifying for admission to the ranks of the good poor. Having read fifteen or twenty volumes of Dickens criticism I have to report that, had it not been for Orwell's essay, this unconscionable drudgery would have been totally without profit. Unfortunately Orwell's article (unlike the books of Professor A and Dr. B) failed to make a 'contribution to knowledge', otherwise it would not be our privilege to read that Dickens was: 'a violent revolutionary', that his 'onslaught on the age is fundamental', that 'not much is left of the established order when he had done with it'. (Walter Allen, *The English Novel*, Phoenix House 1960, p. 159). Perhaps a nation gets the revolutionary heroes it deserves.

2 We cannot go into the reasons for the amazing aplomb with which the English nineteenth-century novelists ignored the unbelievable barbarism of the factory system. Two considerations would probably be fundamental: the non-doctrinaire evolutionism of the working class which had matured too early to be able to profit from the work of the great socialist thinkers, so that the defeat at Peterloo led to a discouragement from which it never recovered. Secondly, there was the formation of a unique oligarchy of 'merchant-aristocrats' which combined the worst qualities of both classes so that the callous stupidity of the entrepreneur came to be sanctioned not only by religion and economic 'law', but by breeding as well.

dispenses with plain common sense and human sympathy than with identity; so that if our thesis is valid, Dickens's superiority must be seen to consist in some kind of refinement or enrichment of identity which will not be effected from the outside by filling in the environment as in Balzac, nor from the inside as in Joyce and in James. But first there are a number of more general issues we will have to discuss.

In his *Système des Beaux-Arts* (the chapter entitled *Du Roman*) Alain remarks: '. . . what is fictional in the novel is not so much the story as that analytical link which causes actions to develop out of thoughts. In real life this never happens.' What we call high-brow art realizes this and therefore will usually restrict itself to one or the other, the inner world (James . . .) or the outer (realism . . .), while art for the masses throws a bridge from one to the other, but at the cost of rendering both absurd; for when action follows from thought (on the level of the *individual,* which is that of the novel) it can only do so because 'thought' has become identity (goodness or badness) which 'naturally' produces its 'action' (reward or retribution).

Dickens undoubtedly belongs at the source of contemporary low-brow art. He was the first of a great tribe who have since given the public exactly 'what it wanted'. And yet, increasingly, from Shaw and Gissing to Edmund Wilson, the cultivated public has been chided for looking upon Dickens as children's reading, and it has become common to find his name joined to that of Shakespeare! So we appear to be concerned with a writer who is at once the great-grandad of soap opera,[3] and a figure to be regarded as 'looming large in the literature of the West' (Wilson).

We will have to deal with this paradox, bearing in mind that James also has been 'looming large' since the last war, and that the ugliest of women may have beautiful hands, but that this should not be enough to get us into bed with her.

---

3 On the explicit as well as implicit levels. For popular entertainment by no means abandons the explicit (thus we should not hang the wrong horse-thief), it stultifies it by always using the 'kind of person' approach; so that the racist is 'evil' to be sure, but nothing is said of the society without which he would not exist in the first place—nothing is said of the breeding ground of the disease.

The explicit content of the novel must, of course, be distinguished from the idiosyncratic. This is of special importance for us since our concern is the novel as a manifestation of cultural structure and not Dickens as a personality. One of the most striking things in Dickens, however, is the extent to which the personal and the social are at one; his only risk was that of neglect, he could never have been misunderstood. The fact that so many of Dickens's heroines are little women would seem clearly to be something personal. And yet, to turn one's heroines into children (Little Nell is a child, Dora is a 'child-bride', Little Dorrit is a woman, but one continually mistaken for a child . . .) is to desexualize them, an operation of which Victorian society could not fail to approve. Dickens's good characters always keep their surroundings neat and clean; he was himself phenomenally tidy;[4] but again, such traits are the translation into private conduct of the general 'rationalization' of life which the industrious bourgeoisie gradually succeeded in imposing. Neatness and cleanliness are indispensable to full efficiency, and we should not forget that Dickens's career was one of the most sensational success stories of the time. (Apart from his novel writing, he quickly became the most efficient of the parliamentary reporters.) But most of Dickens's tidy people are not only not successful, they are very poor, they are the good poor; that is to say those who sell out to their betters by accepting the contradictory and hypocritical proposition of the bourgeoisie: everyone has a fully creditable identity provided he is willing to prove it; which of course meant, in practice, dissociating himself entirely from the great unwashed. You do not need money, the Victorian poor were told, to be clean and tidy, to have *self*-respect. Coming from people with money, this meant in effect: my money has nothing to do with my election, there are no rich or poor, but only the good and the bad, the deserving and the undeserving. This is part of the implicit content of Dickens's

---

4 So that we may get along more quickly I shall take for granted the reader's familiarity not only with Dickens's novels, but with Edgar Johnson's biography. In the present instance, for example, Johnson tells of one of Dickens's sons who, having been apprehended by his father brushing his coat inside rather than outside the house, was careful not to make that mistake a second time.

novels; but in his own life, the master of Gadshill always had an eye for his purse.

It will be objected that it was precisely the 'rationalization of life' that Dickens attacked in the Gradgrind philosophy. But *Hard Times* is one of Dickens's least successful novels because this time he sets out to attack an evil for which efficiency was no cure, on the contrary. Dickens's reformism, and that of nineteenth-century England in general, was the British version of the French Revolution; in other words, it was usually aimed at doing away with the inefficiency of an aristocratic administration (whose bungling of the Crimean War was such that something obviously had to be done) lingering on into an industrial age. The alternative to what Dickens criticized was immediately apparent to the reader—better sanitary conditions, abolition of debtors' prisons (the Marshalsea, incidentally, had already gone when *Little Dorrit* was written), the arrest of brutal schoolmasters, reform of the legal system, etc. In *Hard Times*, however, Dickens encounters a cause rather than a symptom; in this case, modern empiricism with its cast-iron head full of inorganic nightmares. There was consequently no alternative to offer *itself;* so Dickens offered the circus people, a 'return to nature' which in one form or another was that of the entire nineteenth century opposing the abuse of reason with nostalgia rather than with the new dialectical reason created by Hegel and Marx.

For an interesting example of the way in which efficiency works in our society one should consult P. Collins's *Dickens and Crime* (Macmillan, 1962, Chapter 3), where we are given an account of how Coldbath Fields prison was reformed in a manner which gave much satisfaction to Dickens. One of the improvements consisted in forbidding the prisoners to talk to one another. 'Warders', Collins explains, 'had to be with the prisoners, therefore, night and day, watching for any infringement of the rules' (p. 58). These of course were so frequent that punishment 'unfortunately' became far more common than under the old 'inefficient' system. Luckily the governor—and Dickens also—' . . . defended flogging as "beneficial—nay, as indispensable", as well as the treadmill and other forms of useless hard labour' (p. 64). The interesting thing about the system of Coldbath Fields is the way in which

110

it reproduced in miniature bourgeois society at large; for the only way in which a prisoner could be completely successful in never speaking to his fellows was by ceasing to regard them as human beings. In many mills of that day workers were forbidden to talk to one another. It is as though there were a wish to force workers and prisoners to treat each other as they were treated by their betters. The bourgeois dreads solidarity (this is America's fear of Cuba) and he always combats it in the same way, by suppressing subjects (with wishes, fears, goals, etc.) to the advantage of objects with identifications.

Needless to say Dickens the social reformer alienated no one, for the aim of reformism is to *preserve* the system, not to transform it in any fundamental way. It is striking, for example, that whenever Dickens brings up the question of the London slums (of which his descriptions fell far short of the reality) one gets the impression that the chief objection was the way in which they endangered the health of people living in the other sections of the city. Esther's illness which she contracts from Joe the slum child in *Bleak House* is part of the implicit (and therefore most telling) content of the novel, whereas the life and death of Joe is recounted with the usual explicitness, ponderously ironic or sentimental. On Dickens's great billiard table there is a pocket marked 'prison' in which all the black balls come to rest; and therefore not only can there be no question of abolition, reform can easily be carried too far, as it is in the prison visited by David Copperfield where, scandalously, Littimer and Heep are not receiving a punishment befitting their crimes.[5] There are two kinds of reformer;

5 We must not laugh at Dickens's stage villains (Blandois in *Little Dorrit* is so 'evil' that Gowan is able only with the greatest difficulty to keep his dog from springing at him) for his attitude is apparently shared by Lionel Trilling who writes in his preface to *Little Dorrit:* 'Because Blandois exists, prisons are necessary'. One would suppose that the social and mental 'sciences' had had time to establish at least that the hardened criminal, unless he is mentally deficient or psychotic, is a product of the prisons (one need only read Jean Genet's *Miracle de la Rose* to be convinced of this) which are in turn the institutions of a *particular* society. This does not abolish individual responsibility; on the contrary it *establishes* that of eminent professors. The view of Dickens and Trilling amounts to saying: 'I am *in essence* different from you'; and it constitutes the only possible justification for one of the most repellent novels I have ever read, Cozzens's *The Just*

one wants simply to abolish unnecessary suffering, the chief concern of the other is 'justice'. The 'deserving' should not indiscriminately suffer with the 'undeserving',[6] for that involves a confusion of identity which, if it went too far, could bring into question the fitness of the whole Order. Dickens, as Orwell remarked, was an authoritarian, and as such he belongs to the second category. There is something disagreeably ambiguous about the regularity with which Dickens visited prisons wherever he went (he was far less interested in factories which, even in *Hard Times*, we see only from the outside) for there is the question as to how much satisfaction he may have found in observing at close quarters an institution he no doubt regarded as a sort of sewer for keeping the body politic clean, as whore houses are said to protect the 'purity' of 'decent' women. The bourgeois obsession with proving a socially acceptable identity would be meaningless were it not possible to have an identity wrong beyond reclaim, and this is the function of the criminal in our society. The putting forward of an unqualified good, or virtue, instantly establishes evil and sin where they did not exist before. Given a system in which no one is responsible for the public realm because it is the domain of natural 'law', the only way to deal with the various social evils is to incarnate them in certain evil individuals who can then be imprisoned or destroyed. The scapegoat is therefore vital to bourgeois society because through him

---

and the Unjust, in which the author is outraged that two criminals (whose trial takes up a large part of the novel) should have been given considerably less than the maximum penalty by a jury forgetful, presumably, that it was an instrument of divine justice.

6 We learn from Johnson (Vol. II, p. 610) that at the conclusion of a lunch which had brought together Dickens and some friends, it was decided that a number of the left-over sandwiches should be distributed to the poor. The servant placed in charge of this operation was directed by Forster to inquire into the 'life, conduct and behaviour' of his candidates. Dickens himself would have been amused by this, but it is sobering to think that this noble Victorian was Dickens's closest friend throughout the greater part of his life. Dickens, furthermore, was always very sensitive to the reproach that the 'undeserving' might easily benefit from some of the reforms he advocated. On his way to help some orphaned children, the good Jarndyce in *Bleak House* (Chapter XV) stops to ask the way, and at the same time inquires whether the father had been industrious. Had the answer been 'no', would the sins of the parent have been visited upon the children? Perhaps, since Esther, in the same novel, talks about her 'heritage of shame'.

the impression may be given that the public realm is being effectively controlled (whereas, of course, it is being used to augment the private) and because his existence helps to establish the inmost region of the private realm—the self—as respectable.[7]

The extent to which Dickens's reformism worked within the order of his day may be judged by the fact that he fully sub-subscribed to that choice Victorian hypocrisy—the alleged identity of interests between 'masters and men'.[8]

Dickens in no way transcended his period; his genius was of a different nature: it permitted him to construct a mythical world so compelling that *moral law seemed able to cohabit there with political and social chaos.*

With Dickens we can have our cake and eat it too. He can even suggest, as in *Little Dorrit,* that the world might be a prison. But what of that? Malthus had gone much further to suggest that starvation itself was part of the Great Plan. All we ask is that the world be *unalterably given* so that there can be no question of our personal responsibility. And what kind of prison life is it that is shared with a representative from another world—Little Dorrit in the Marshalsea? Another world which not only grants us permanent envoys, but which takes a hand now and then whenever necessary, as in the collapse of the Clenham house. To eliminate as unessential naïveties such aspects of Dickens's work is to cut out its under-lying *raison d'être*; its implicit content, that portion of the novel we *experience*, that portion which made it psychologically practicable for Dickens to be relatively outspoken in other respects.

In the works of his maturity, Dickens gives the impression of a

---

7 I think the immense popularity of detective novels could probably be explained along these lines. If the puzzle element were uppermost, they could just as well be about clever thefts (or many other things) rather than, as is almost always the case, the way in which a *murderer* is apprehended. The detective story is not a parasitical off-shoot but a 'simplification' to which the novel tends by its very nature. In so far as the novel identifies, it invites the reader to sit in judgment; why not, then, facilitate his work by offering him the *indubitable* criminality of the killer? The 'respectable' are those who yearn to judge. Like Dickens, therefore, they will be much interested by crime.

8 See Johnson, Vol. I, pp. 574 and 582.

world darkling under the effects of some congenital corruption and *simultaneously* conveys an absolute reassurance. This latter is almost always part of the implicit content, but Dickens occasionally slips up and comes right out with it, as in *Little Dorrit*, where he tells how the heart of John Chivery '. . . swelled to the size of the heart of a gentleman; and the poor common little fellow . . .'[9] This remark, which expresses Dickens's inmost feelings, is in direct contradiction with what, on the explicit level, much of the novel is about—the tragi-comic consequences of social pretension; and this contradiction is one that Dickens attempts to resolve in all his novels because he had to resolve it in his own life. I refer, of course, to his several months in a blacking factory as a child and, though it was considerably less important, his father's incarceration for debt. We have seen that the bourgeois is engaged in proving an identity which at the same time he must regard as given, and if we wish to understand why this brief period in Dickens's life should have been traumatic, we must look upon it as casting doubt upon his identity *as an essence* which, as such, should not be subject to revocation by circumstance; but since human 'objectivity' is not immediately and therefore indubitably given in consciousness, how can we be sure this revocation has not taken place, or that identity is not, in reality, a mere being-for-others?

What gives Dickens's famous letter to Forster its weight is less the dreadful emphasis than the fact that the incident he reveals was kept from his own family, who learned of it only after his death. What was it that haunted him throughout his life to such an extent; for, as Freud has taught us, it is what we refuse to have out in the open that best accounts for the irrational intricacies of character. For many years Dickens avoided the streets close to the factory where he had worked, less they remind him of '. . . what I once was', and what he once was he states in the same letter: '. . . I know that I worked, from morning to night, with common men and boys . . .'. The horror of the experience was that (though for

---

9 Page 219. All page references are to the New Oxford Illustrated Dickens. In *Bleak House* (p. 507) Esther is surprised to find: '. . . this nobility in the soul of a labouring man's daughter'.

a period of less than six months) he had been almost in-distinguishable from a 'common boy'.

It is as though the novels were a long attempt to eradicate this incident by asserting that identity is an absolute about which there is no possibility of error either on the part of the person concerned (except in the case of the purely comic characters, in fact this is what makes them funny, as we shall see shortly) or those who know him except (as in the case of Dickens himself) where appearances may temporarily deceive. So it is that no trace of Oliver Twist's milieu ever rubs off on to him, and David Copperfield can be, in a picturesque incident without lasting importance, a labouring gentleman. In other words, identity is a function not of scientific law (that is, of environ-ment, as in French realism) but of moral law. There are, of course, many passages in which Dickens points out to 'England's honourable lords and gentlemen' that slums breed criminals as well as disease; but again the distinction between explicit and implicit content must not be forgotten, for Oliver Twist (and, to a considerable extent, Nancy and the Dodger in the same book) is no more remarkable a case than Lizzie Hexam or Amy Dorrit or Pip along with a host of the 'good poor'. To return to the billiard ball analogy, most of Dickens's characters move over their various surfaces having a minimum of contact with it. It is not the surface which is the determining factor, but the cue. The last three completed novels contain an additional element which is not, however, an environment, but an atmosphere. The fog in *Bleak House*, the river in *Our Mutual Friend*, the various prisons of *Little Dorrit* are less material than spiritual; they are a *moralized* environment emanating from the characters and providing them with an appropriate living space, but not stamping itself upon them. We have an antici-pation of this technique in *Dombey and Son*, where Dombey's house is described almost entirely in terms having a moral resonance; it is cold, proud, joyless, severe—in other words Dombey himself in different form. If we compare this to Balzac's *César Birotteau*, we see at once that in Balzac's novel there is *interaction* between character and milieu. We learn a great deal about Birotteau's business; about Dombey's we know next to nothing. In Balzac's mind Birotteau is to a great extent the product of commercial conditions in Paris at that particular time. London commerce, inversely, is the product of Dombey and his like; so our attention, naturally, centres on him. Dombey measures himself not against things, not against others in the form of the *pratico-inerte*, but against another identity—his daughter Florence. The material world of Dickens has no 'coefficient of adversity', it moves about with his characters as they move their limbs, it is an *extension of identity*. No need for sordid bargaining when the partnership of Doyce and Clenham is formed in *Little Dorrit* because each infallibly knew the other and because in Dickens there is no weighty train of things to drag a character in a direction incompatible with his identity (Dickens is at pains to make Clenham's responsibility for the bankruptcy quite slight, and it all turns out well in the long run anyway). The Circumlocution Office is simply the collective identity of the Barnacles, as the Court of Chancery is that of the 'symbolic' Krook, Miss Flite, Kenge, Vholes, etc.[10] The novel tends to represent the objects amid which we live as far more inert than they really are. In real life we use them, but they also *resist*; usually to the point of compelling us to change direction more often than we should wish. This seldom happens in Dickens however (except of course in the case of evil characters who are thwarted by things which have become instruments of the beyond); the deadly travail of existence takes place off stage so that it will not interfere with the pre-ordained criss-crossed trajectories of the actors. Think, for example, of the preposterous test to which Bella Wilfer is subjected in *Our Mutual Friend* to determine whether she is a gold-digger—only in the novel can action follow from thought to such perfection; or the nonchalance with which Dickens's characters set out in search of one another as though they were going into the next room (Solomon Gills after Walter Gay; Peggoty after little Emily; Caveletto after Blandois); or the way in which Pancks establishes Dorrit's right to an inheritance, overcoming many difficulties which (as always in Dickens) are simply mentioned, never shown. It may,

10 The reader is aware that these remarks are not altogether a criticism of Dickens, but an illustration of certain 'structural determinisms'. Dickens's social criticisms are as effective as they are because he embodies them in identities. From those capable of it, the novel requires this procedure; from others, we get dismal tracts like Orwell's *Keep the Aspidistra Flying*.

116

however, do us a disservice to cite these examples of the blitheness with which the requirements of identity cause the novelist to ignore the sullen independence of things, for what is important about this characteristic of fiction is that it is so diffuse as to attain that strange invisibility of the too obvious. It is the business of phenomenology to thicken into opaqueness what is so evident as to be transparent (it is not, for example the *way* in which many novelists explore interiority, but the fact that they do so that counts). Structure can then help us decide which of the elements we have managed to 'bring into focus' are taking most of the stress. In the present instance, the 'irrealization' of the world around us to which identity leads has an importance one could hardly over-emphasize. It is in mass entertainment that the coefficient of adversity of things has been reduced most nearly to nothing—it presents a world which is unresistingly *ours*; one which, in other words, no longer exists.

The heroes of Dickens are the direct translation into fiction of the moral law. They are the public realm in terms of identity; the result being that identity in these cases ceases to have anything personal about it at all. The 'good' in Dickens are absolutely interchangeable because they are simply the moral law in operation. There is no introspection, no perplexity, only reflex action; only a standard against which to measure the comic or the evil. Low-brow fiction often advertises itself as being taken from 'real life'—crime stories will be based upon the 'files of. . .', magazines are full of 'true romance', and this answers a pathetic need (shared by philosophers in so far as they are in quest of an ethical *system*) to believe in the practicability of automatic moral responses. Can we in all circumstances and unreflectingly be honest, chaste, truthful, and so forth without making damn fools of ourselves? Dickens answers with an unqualified yes. We all know, however, that virtue is not rewarded, and one of the functions of the bourgeois ethic of intention is to overcome this difficulty. Whatever the practical effect of our action, if the intention is good we can be at peace with ourselves, virtue is its own reward; and this principle applies of course also to those whose role is a public one, with the inevitable sacrifice of the public to the private realm which makes the white man less than useless wherever he puts his mind to the problems of the underdeveloped world.[11] Except at moments of crisis, an advanced economy is carried along partly by its own momentum, so that public servants can get on without *showing results* if their intentions are those of the right kind of individual. There exists, however, a corps of public servants—the Objective Society—which has succeeded in forgetting that it is in any sense public at all; or rather, as in the case of Dickens's good characters, these people embody the public realm as individuals through purity of intention. Their 'public' service is simply to achieve and then pass on the right attitudes, so that even on the intellectual level no practical results are expected or required (on the contrary) apart from research—which is the revealing of aspects of the public realm—the successful pursuit of which requires simply an attitude: objectivity. Dickens's heroes, however, are not public servants, so that the reward of their virtue cannot consist in a release from responsibility thanks to innocence of intention; nor can it take the form of the 'after life', since no one really believes in it any longer (except people like the Africans who, however, are being converted to unbelief by missionary education); nor, except for the phoney, can there be 'peace with oneself', since the self is not an entity, but a 'direction'. In brief, by seeing to it that virtue is handsomely and concretely rewarded, Dickens is having the courage of the system. A culture which has sacrificed *both* the here and now (by equating the 'we' with the mob) and the hereafter (fallen from perception to 'knowledge') is exposed to despair and the absurd unless it clings child-like, with Dickens and mass culture, to its notion of a sanctified identity. Whenever Dickens brings in the hereafter his prose swells and rolls, sometimes spilling over into blank verse because the subject needs a little

---

11 Stalinists try to do something about this by arguing that, however good the intention, if the result is such as to harm the greater number, then *objectively* it is to be condemned. But one doesn't break out of bourgeois ideology by shifting from subject to object, since it is this division which constitutes its very essence. All one achieves is an 'inverse identity', consciousness as 'reflection'; for how can the Stalinist know infallibly, as he claims to, what word or act favours or harms the cause of the proletariat unless he possesses the key to history? And if such a key exists, then consciousness is epiphenomenal.

help.[12] Identity, on the contrary, though it is simply the reverse of the coin, can be taken for granted;[13] and this is the confusion which has enabled our culture to strike a pose of scepticism and rationality while accepting, lock, stock and barrel, the system as it stands. It has even caused Dickens to be taken for a 'rebel' by no less a critic than Edmund Wilson. The quality of his rebellion may be judged from an episode in *Little Dorrit*. William Dorrit has come into a fortune and his daughter Amy wonders for a moment that he should be expected both to pay his debts and suffer twenty years imprisonment. Why, indeed, should he pay twice over? But what appears a perfectly reasonable attitude on Amy's part is instead, according to Dickens, evidence that poor Little Dorrit had been 'tainted' (ever so slightly of course) by her residence in the Marshalsea. Luckily Clenham is present and keeps the rot from getting a foothold with the usual moral-reflex of the good character. One *always* pays one's debts. The 'impersonal', 'objective' moral law of which the good character is the embodiment is here seen to be what it is in reality, a part of the bourgeois ethic, and in the present case, of the sacredness of money. Money is more sacred than love since Clenham, having become a pauper, is unable to marry Little Dorrit who is rich. A similar situation arises at the end of *Martin Chuzzlewit*. The keys which Esther jangles proudly and happily from one end to the other of *Bleak House*, strike me as a far more significant symbol than the fog, if we must talk of symbols. Simone Weil would leave what money she had on a mantelpiece near her door so that people going by could take what they needed. Strange that such a proceeding should be inconceivable at Bleak House where everyone, nevertheless, was so kind-hearted (at least toward the 'deserving'). Esther's exemplary Christianity should strike us as being in poor accord with her basket of keys. If

12 In a letter to his son, Dickens recommends religion for its comfort-giving qualities. Such is religion in bourgeois society—less a conviction than a sedative.

13 Dickens one day discovered that some faithful old servant had been stealing from him, and he wrote: 'It has so shocked me that I have had to walk more than usual before I could walk myself into composure again' (Johnson, Vol. II, p. 1066). He had good cause to be shocked, for what becomes of the world of his novels when we acknowledge that people are both 'good' and 'bad'; in other words neither, like this servant.

Dickens intended that the name Merdle should suggest the word *merde*, we must not suppose he also intended: money= *merde*. Merdle inspires an extraordinary loathing in Dickens not because he represents the disastrous omnipotence of money, but because he defiled the Temple, tampered with a sacred institution. (Characters like Skimpole and Gowan, who take a cavalier attitude toward money, are severely dealt with by Dickens.) Had Dickens wanted to hint that money is comparable to excrement, he had a wonderful opportunity to do so in *Our Mutual Friend* where the words 'dust heap' are a euphemism; but no gentleman would have left his readers in the contemplation of a hero and heroine living happily ever after on the proceeds of *merde*.

Of all Dickens's good characters, Pip of *Great Expectations* is the only one to offer any complexity. The usual transparent medium, with a first and last name as its only individuality, through which the beyond of morality is refracted into daily life, becomes somewhat clouded. Pip, for a while, undergoes the temptation of snobbery. Does this mean that in *Great Expectations* Dickens deals honestly with the problem upon which he had turned his back in *David Copperfield?* Is he saying, however hesitantly and indirectly, in this second novel in the first person that the unbridgeable gulf he had placed between the little gentleman and the 'common men and boys' in the blacking factory was pure snobbery on his part?

We know that one of the basic cultural contradictions of bourgeois society is the necessity of proving an identity which must, nevertheless, be regarded as given. We have also seen that 'culture' is the most satisfying solution; but for Dickens, as for the great majority, the problem resolves itself into determining the relationship between identity and money. The simple evidence (which we find expressed in Stendhal) is that identity is a being-for-others absolutely dependent upon whatever form of display happens to be required by the group concerned. But our society has always been rich in propaganda hinting that money is far less important than it may appear ('you can't buy happiness', 'best things in life are free', etc.), which in fact is meant to suggest that identity is an endowment; it is given, and not acquired by money or in any other way. The bourgeois lives with the nostalgic regret of an identity (which was that of the aristocracy) of which wealth would be an *inessential* outward sign; an identity securely and indubitably possessed; in other words an object with the inexplicable power of self-contemplation. Pip is unique among Dickens's heroes for having entertained a doubt (due partly to youth, partly to his hopeless love for Estelle) as to his identity[14] which took the form of supposing it to be connected with money, and his punishment was the discovery that he owed his great expectations to a convict. On the explicit level at least, money is a veneer (the *nouveaux riches* of *Our Mutual Friend* are called the Veneerings) and one does not, as Pip momentarily believed, become one of the elect by such means. The true role of money, since it is sacred (implicit content) is to enable the beyond to acknowledge an election. No 'good' character in Dickens ever suffers from want for long. Martin Chuzzlewit, about to go hungry, receives money from an unknown benefactor; Mrs. Nickleby and Kate, though in dire straits, have a servant; Clenham, having refused money (that offered by Little Dorrit) is immediately released from the debtors' prison and placed in a position to make a comfortable living, etc., etc. Clenham could no more have taken Little Dorrit's money than he could have taken her blood. Money is so blessed that there is something monstrous in having it apart from merit. Such people threaten the Order and are dealt with accordingly—Dombey is brought low, aristocrats are ridiculous (money by inheritance), speculators (Merdle) commit suicide, and part of Bounderby's villainy is that he was far less self-made than he claimed to be. Money which he had done nothing to merit brings only trouble to Pip, whereas he lives happily ever after thanks to his partnership with Herbert who owed his prosperity to an early and secret gift of money from Pip. Dickens, consequently, saddles himself with one of the sorriest of

---

14 A doubt which is absurd, since his accent is altogether different from that of the people who brought him up—an anomaly to be accounted for only in terms of the bourgeois myth of election. We can appreciate here why the difference between Dickens and Dostoevsky (who are sometimes compared) is almost one of kind, since the identity of many of the characters of Dostoevsky consists precisely in the fact that they are unable to achieve one; they are consumed by a doubt which it was one of the main purposes of Dickens's art to dispel.

bourgeois hypocrisies—that according to which money does not constitute identity, it sanctions it.

The gentleman is a contradictory amalgam of aristocratic endowment and bourgeois morality (in other words, as we said, he is an identity which has to be proven). It is moral to earn money, but gentility is not arrived at except in so far as the whole question is suppressed. Money is like salt in food; it must be there, but equally important, we must not be aware of it. It is where money can be turned into 'culture' that it is most successfully passed off as acknowledgment of election. Bourgeois culture is money absorbed into the substance of the self; hence the curious affectation of effortlessness to be found at Oxbridge. Examinations have to be passed and lectures prepared (just as money may have to be earned) but everything is done to minimize the importance of this below-stairs aspect of university life.[15]

From the first appearance of *The Pickwick Papers* to the present Dickens has enjoyed a popularity unexampled in our literature. He consequently answered a need (although he also of course contributed to determining its exact nature), and one which is more than ever with us today in the form of an insatiable market for low-brow art; it is a need inseparable from bourgeois culture and should consequently form part of the immediate, subjective experience of each of us.

The difficulty is that no one is much concerned about Dickens any longer except the cultivated, and culture, which is that part of classical reason in charge of things aesthetic, is not intended to come to grips with subjective experience, but to free us from its importunities. Like reason, it is the measuring rod which is never itself measured. It cannot regard itself as a *comportment* the purpose of which is to provide a warm cocoon for lay souls, any more than reason can be brought to see that it helps constitute a world it then regards as a discovery. Culture, like reason, separates itself from, in order to possess in full; in so far as it is academic, it is part of what Merleau-Ponty called *la pensée de survol*. The higher we are, the more we can

15 In *The Long Revolution*, Raymond Williams tells of being present while each of three Oxford dons, one after the other, explained before a class of foreigners that he knew nothing about the subject and had, in any case, forgotten his lecture notes.

encompass, and since knowledge operates 'at a distance', this is equivalent to 'possessing' more. The life of the mind will consist largely in identifying (knowing) what is possessed; and this identification is regarded as a *necessary preliminary to any valid experience of*. . . My appreciation of the work of Dickens will depend upon an 'identification', but one so complex that I could not be criticized for never arriving at it. In the meantime it is 'approached' through the increasing stock of information provided by the researchers.

In fact, however, learning about Dickens serves to conceal an underlying experience without which no one would have dreamed of learning about Dickens. The information acquired does not clarify or enrich the initial experience, it *replaces* with knowledge, the common undertaking (or 'need') of Dickens and his readers. The natural sequence is reversed. The knowledge does not make possible the experience; on the contrary, it is thanks to the experience that the knowledge is sought, much as we possess our native tongue and only subsequently acquire knowledge of its grammar.

Since Wilson's article 'The Two Scrooges', anyone writing on Dickens has had to dwell upon the symbol question, but of course this has nothing to do with Dickens's immense popularity which preceded the appearance of most of these symbols in his mature work. A preoccupation with formal values, techniques, etc., is a secondary approach to art; it does not reveal the 'secrets' of an artist's greatness; it confuses objective criteria with essential nature, just as nineteenth-century scientism confused measurability with the 'true nature' of objects. The scholars say that since we have come to know of Dickens's relationship with Ellen Ternan, much light is thrown upon the later novels. What this means in reality is that objects of experience may eventually be transformed into objects of knowledge. With the passage of jazz from the back streets of southern cities where it was an 'article of consumption', where it was 'lived' by a given social group, to the Newport Festivals, where it is an 'object of contemplation', a radical change in the nature and function of jazz has taken place. No one presumably would argue that Newport concert-goers, since they know so much more about jazz, have a deeper and more satisfying commerce with it than had the people for whom it was originally intended; all that can be said is that the former, having placed themselves at a distance, can *talk about* jazz, while experience is usually dumb; just as talk about sex is often a substitute for it. An ethnologist may have a comprehensive knowledge of African sculpture and yet his understanding of it will be superficial compared to that of a man who succeeds (to the extent in which this is possible) in sharing the life of a single African tribe. To put this differently, the ethnologist, in extending his investigations, is not getting at the truth about African sculpture, he is *creating* an object of knowledge. The 'objective' point of view brings into being its own specific reality which, since it is divorced by principle from our daily lives, can be wearisome to an extreme. One has only to watch the faces of the Sunday afternoon museum visitors living life on a 'higher plane', trying to add to their lives as a substitute for transforming them, acquiring instead of doing. Only the artist does not get weary in the galleries, because he is utilizing them; because he is not trying to possess the art of the past *in itself*. His is a 'narrow', 'partisan' (if he is a good artist), 'subjective' approach. He 'negates' past art with the help of his own endeavours, and so gives it the only voice it can have.

The *Pickwick Papers* and *Nicholas Nickleby* in particular give the impression of a gay tune struck up by a theatre orchestra leader because smoke has begun to appear from behind the scenes. The England of the chartist movement could be compared to the South Africa of today (unless we commit the 'retrospective error' of assuming that because there was no revolution in the 1840s there had never been any danger of it) and South Africa is full of whites who simply 'cannot understand' the concern felt by the outsider over the situation there. In other words, conditions are such that the white man *cannot* face them honestly and continue to live as before; instead he will talk of what a wonderful human being the African is, of how much loyalty the visitor fails to see and, in any case, changes will eventually be brought about by constitutional means. That loyal, grateful African is none other than Dickens's 'family retainer' type of which Sam Weller was the first; and we touch here upon the idyllic class relationship which exists where the disruptive notion of social class has been dismissed with the contempt it deserves. Instead there is the familiar planetarium of monads, all equal, but occupying different ranks; with this *douce égalité* (as we found Rousseau expressing it) taking the form of the great tact and kindness with which the 'less fortunate' are treated by the 'more fortunate'. The one obstacle to this happy arrangement is, of course, the existence of malcontents, of the 'bad poor'[16] who are at the source of all social unrest and against whom, therefore, the very harshest measures are often the best advised. This contrast between the extreme brutality with which malcontents and lesser breeds may be treated and the great kindness usually to be found in personal relationships is one of the curiosities of our culture. There were the Nazi exterminators who were often excellent fathers and husbands; there is the courteous English animal lover campaigning for the return of corporal punishment in prisons and schools; the warm-hearted, friendly American fighting the war in Vietnam and eager to annihilate the Chinese with atomic bombs. The author of *Oliver Twist* was also a man who, in the company of Mark Lemon, one day triumphantly collared a pick-pocket after a chase through the streets. Years later, the same Christmassy gentleman insisted, before a reluctant magistrate, that a young woman be sent to jail for having used 'foul language'.[17]

We decided, it will be recalled, that the 'art of event' is more real, more concrete than bourgeois representational art. Renaissance tragedy stands between the two; it is based upon fact like the former; but, like the latter, it is also concerned with

---

16 The well-to-do Englishman, questioned about social relationships in his country, will usually explain that it is the resentment of some of the poorer elements of the population which keeps the whole nasty caste system in existence. If you then inquire why the public schools are not abolished you learn that there is no point, since they would simply move to Ireland!—an excellent example of the way in which the 'materiality' of our society (which, as we have seen, *is* the dominant social class) can be regarded as a given which will be either insuperable (realism) or which will lend itself to the most extravagant requirements of identity (mass entertainment).

17 See *Dickens and Crime*, p. 113. In the improbable event of a Dickensian being distressed by this revelation, Collins points out that in the London of the day, Dickens's act was 'sensible and public spirited'. I'm afraid Collins proves only that for as long as there are academics ready with their wealth of historical knowledge to help us understand things of this kind we shall need that young woman's dirty words.

the representation of character. The tragedies of Racine and Shakespeare recount events the authenticity of which no contemporary would have dreamed of contesting. This reality was so indubitable that a great 'irreality' of presentation was possible—use of verse, stage conventions, etc. In the novel, by contrast, the *imaginary* nature of the events had to be compensated for by the utmost reality of presentation—use of prose, of people and scenes of everyday life, etc. The preoccupation with form, so typical of classicism, marks an effort to give uncontested and quasi-sacred event or idea an expression worthy of it. The novel, however, does not enshrine or commemorate, it seeks to render plausible, to create the illusion of reality. And yet, to achieve this end, the art of fiction, the art of the great practical, hard-headed, empirical bourgeoisie is carried on with no less than three purely *imaginary* realities: story, character, and the moral they point which, however valid within the confines of the particular novel, can never apply to *my* unique and unjustifiable existence here and now. The novelist, in undertaking to show a *putative* higher reality by means of the *imaginary* dispenses with the guide lines and exposes himself to the temptations of creating an art of persuasion, of special pleading. The novel is by nature impure; it had in it from the beginning the seeds of mass entertainment. It is a 'hypocritical' art in that it purports simply to show, whereas in fact it militates for 'universality'; or, to put it differently, it 'shows' the invisible, the merely known.

Consider what Dickens overlooked in every dialogue he wrote—the fact that people undergo astonishing transformations depending upon the company in which they find themselves, there may even in some instances be a slight change of accent. The novel, as we know, is about the alleged constants which underly these transformations; but not only are such constants *not* there 'ontologically' as the bourgeois would wish, to assert them implies the *elimination of the other*.[18] Dialogue in Dickens resembles those animated electric signs in which the bulbs are alternately lit and extinguished. Susan

18 This can take various forms. It can be absolute, as in *Robinson Crusoe* and the many modern novels of self-communion and self-display or otherness may disappear in a 'harmony of essences' which makes talk superfluous, as in 'perfect' love and friendship.

126

Nipper is able to tell off Dombey exactly as she would do in imagination, as though Dombey *were not there*. But in actual fact she would have been incapable of such a speech even to herself, certainly not in the presence of the formidable Dombey, her employer, even had he allowed her to finish; so that in order to show Susan's identity (she is one of the many beneath-that-gruff-exterior types to be found in Dickens) in action, Dickens sets himself at three removes from the plainest reality. Trotty Beck, in *The Chimes*, is an ageing man who works as a 'ticket porter' (i.e. an errand boy). This involves his standing outside in all weather until beckoned to by some gentleman of Dickens's station in life. The reader learns that Trotty 'loves to earn his money' (as do all the 'deserving poor') so that when, two or three pages further along, Dickens speaks of the 'dignity of labour', the resulting confusion is not evidence that Dickens was born with a lesser genius than Stendhal, but that, in dealing with the social problems of his time, he had remained at one with the convenient vision of his class which regards the essential relationship as that which links a man with some aspect of the beyond rather than with his fellows. According to Dickens the beyond looked after the deserving poor, according to Malthus it destroyed them. Take your pick. What really matters is the absurdity of using the expression 'dignity of labour' in reference to people who not only accept their degradation but are proud of it (if they are deserving) because their society has mystified them into supposing that they are entities of a given kind. No writer of antiquity would have spoken of the dignity of slave labour, because slaves were part of the plunder of war, victims of superior force and cunning. So were the nineteenth-century poor (and, of course, the modern consumer), but with the coming of the industrial revolution the whole weight of bourgeois rationalism was thrown into an attempt to obscure this fact. A metaphysics which had fought a long war of liberation became an instrument of oppression, and the novel marks this reconversion.

It is not easy even now to realize how very peculiar is the reality which the novel, and especially that of Dickens, presents to us. We have already spoken of the God's-eye view which the novelist adopts and which enables him to describe a *supposed* reality which he imagines is *visual*, or at least knowable in one way or another. In thinking of the Dickensian dialogue it is easier to see how even the most 'indispensable' constituents of an art are related to the way of life of the society to which the artist belongs. These elements are indispensable in the sense that they have got to 'fit in' to the cultural structure in question, and yet this 'fitting in' becomes increasingly motivated in proportion as it is obliged to omit or distort areas of reality which have grown in importance. For example, we can see *now* what the Renaissance artist left out (life, as opposed to life *for an observer*) to relate his figures to a vanishing point (to turn them into objects) rather than to himself. But of course this procedure was in its time a great achievement playing a vital role in the gestation of the scientific vision of the universe. When Dickens takes it up, however, its artificiality is more apparent. Why did he attach no importance to the obvious fact that our 'natures' undergo wild fluctuations depending upon the people we are with? In Dickens's novels each character, as he speaks, comes to the front of the stage while the others sink into darkness, they *disappear*, while light falls upon the thread of identity stretching into infinity where there reigns an Order through which all interpersonal communication must pass. We are not often enough aware of how extraordinary a paradox is involved here. The reader is a watcher at the window (that is, he peeks in upon reality as it 'really is') knowing perfectly well that the spectacle has been carefully arranged for him by the novelist. If the reader is so uncouth as to take the after-all-it's-only-a-story attitude he will be called to order by Forster in a passage already quoted, reminding him that from the novel we get '. . . a reality of a kind we can never get in daily life'. The uncouth reader should nevertheless stick to his guns and insist that the parallel with pre-cubist art holds good: the 'higher' reality to which Forster refers, an aspect of which the orthodox artist was able to capture thanks to the 'discovery' of perspective (moral principle for the novelist), as a matter of fact depends absolutely upon the point of view adopted by the painter—alter it, and the picture falls to pieces, the perspective is destroyed. It is the same with the novelist whose higher reality is visible *only* from the peculiar vantage point of his culture and class. When Ruskin writes: 'The Chinese, children of all things, suppose a good perspective drawing to be as false as we feel their plate patterns to be . . .',[19] we recognize at once the ugly bigotry of nineteenth-century scientism with its adventurers and missionaries laying coarse hands upon cultures usually more refined and humane than their own. If we can see how the way leads unbroken from the learned and highly principled Ruskin to the gunboat missionaries and forced labour of colonialism, we should be able to sense a similar connection between the 'objectivation' of man which we find in the novel, and the man-object-of-this-kind-and-hence-to-be-discarded of the twentieth-century concentration camps; between the novel's quest for the truth about human nature, and the Fascist's or racist's claim that this truth is already known.[20] The only possible relationship between identities is cognitive, exterior; so that relations between fictional characters can never be interior, *as they are in real life*. To take an extreme example, no psychoanalyst would suppose that his treatment of a particular case could be facilitated if he were to stay in his patient's home so as to observe his family life at first hand. The patient, knowing himself observed, would, despite all his efforts, become a different person; in fact the effort alone would transform him. Valéry somewhere remarks that a man who writes books may well turn into an author, into something that does not exist; or, to use our familiar term, he may acquire an identity. And yet, it is also the case that this person who writes books may be compelled by those around him to become an author, they need only refuse to forget with whom they have the privilege of speaking; then, any attempt by the 'author' to relapse into humanity is met by the furtive knowing smiles of people aware he is an author. In other words identity, like everything else, is simultaneously projected by us and discovered out there—as though the world were a colossal Rorschach test. The experience of being reified in this way whether into a thief

---

19 Quoted by E. H. Gombrich, *Art and Illusion*, Phaidon, 1960, p. 268.

20 The Nazi concentration camps were carefully organized to maintain and wherever possible increase the 'seriality' which is the basic structure of western capitalist society. The camps would function efficiently for just so long as the administration could prevent the coming-together of men for whom the goal (effective resistance) and their 'individual identity' would be one and the same thing.

or an author, is extremely distressing because it exacerbates the solitude to which we are already condemned by the nature of our society. Our writer of books must be assumed to be one whose entire life is being consumed in the effort he is making; but since this is rarely so, the objectivation which he detests, is eagerly sought by many of those who write; it is the real goal of their efforts. The phoney, therefore, seeks the solitude from which he is going to suffer, for he is terrified of *not being recognized* in that seething mass of partisans; even though there, no one is alone because the self-thing has been supplanted by the 'coalescence' of purpose which, at the moment, and apart from revolutionary groups, is the monopoly of an infinitesimal minority of great scientists, artists, and philosophers.

This solitude of the bourgeois individual which is at once chosen and suffered, is workable only where, given such monads, there is *also* a pre-established harmony. Thus, although Dickens's characters speak in a room where they are alone (otherwise they could not possibly speak in such a way) this does not matter because communication is pre-established, talk simply confirms it.

The absolute dependence of the novel upon a stable Order (which, being hidden, accessible only to knowledge or conscience, can be more or less consciously used for class purposes) [21] the vital aspect of which is, for the novel, the 'objectivity' of human nature, may be judged from the fact that the more scrupulously a novelist depicts everyday reality the less the interest of his work. Thus Moore and Gissing are far more 'real' than Dickens, but also infinitely less readable. A certain 'distortion' is indispensable; one which will 'simplify' human beings, abstract them into intelligibility on the basis of the author's convictions (reasoned or otherwise) as to the 'meaning of life'.

The progress of the novel after Dickens was marked by the elimination of the 'invisible hand' in its more crass manifestations so that the beyond comes to be more closely confined to character alone. Faulkner's characters, for example,

---

21 The superiority of the French nineteenth-century novel over the English derives from its greater emphasis upon the scientific rather than the moral Order. Its elements of persuasion are kept to a minimum.

carry their destiny 'within' them, which makes possible, as with Tolstoy, a better fusion of the implicit and explicit, for the explicit becomes ingrained in the story in the form of character (the implicit). In a book like *Absalom, Absalom!* consequently, Faulkner is able to deal with his problem (racism) in a way more satisfying than Dickens was able to deal with his (the labouring poor and their persecutors) in *Hard Times*. In both cases nevertheless an essentially *reassuring* implicit content remains—it is naïve in Dickens: each of his characters is propelled unerringly by the divine cue into the pocket destined to receive a ball of that particular colour; in Faulkner the balls have become more irregular and complex in contour, and for that reason must be more self-propelled, but we still have 'ontologically' separate entities incapable of losing their separateness and so changing the whole nature of the game.[22] Forster's distinction between flat and round characters in fiction will not do. All Dickens's characters are clear-cut, polished and well-defined, so that if we are to assign a shape to them it should be spherical. Authors who probe more deeply (as the expression has it) do not reach a fuller, more rounded definition, they explode Dickens's brightly coloured billiard balls into shapeless masses more true to life but less true to the novel which is about identity. (It would be hard to imagine anyone more unlike Dickens than Proust, whose great novel is nevertheless full of near-Dickensian characters—Bloch, Norpois, Madame Verdurin, etc.). These novelists do not teach us more about what man *is*, they concentrate upon a *different aspect* of human life, its alleged 'interiority'; but this places them in an awkward position, for their whole enterprise is undertaken on the assumption that human beings have identities susceptible to 'exploration', whereas a man's 'nature' is established *from the outside* and is consequently never wholly justified. (From inside, for ourselves, we are a void; except for the

22 Failing to see that content in the novel *is* its form, many critics have been misled by some of Faulkner's formal experiments (in *The Sound and the Fury*, for example) into supposing him much more of a contemporary than he really was. Such substance as is there derives almost entirely (as in the case of Mérimée) from the juxtaposition of two sets of values: those of the reader, and those of the primitives of Yoknapatawpha County.

phoney who, as we have seen, takes the point of view of the other upon himself.)[23]

The comparison between Dickens and Faulkner is instructive. In each case we have a novelist who (since the novel must show) returns again and again to the basic problem of his society—for Dickens the poor, for Faulkner the Negroes—but who as a *novelist* cannot envisage the only permanent solution: the ideological as well as practical replacement of the individual by the group, for this would lead to a conception of human nature and of reality with which the novel, as it has existed up to the present, would be unable to cope. Hence both novelists are obliged to advocate measures which are not measures at all: in Dickens a change of heart on the part of the wealthy and in Faulkner non-interference from the north in the racial problems of the south. Improvements have to be granted by the privileged and in no circumstances wrested from them. The present Order must be made to work, for the alternative is 'chaos'; i.e. a state of affairs in which *differences* of identity (the substance of the novel) will be seen to be artificial and arbitrary.

One could liken the poor for Dickens and the Negroes for Faulkner to an 'unconscious' which a novelist could never successfully confront and remain the same writer; and yet, of course, it is part of the man himself, there is no avoiding it. This dilemma (which is that of the western liberal since the end of the eighteenth century) is resolved by simultaneously dealing with a problem and leaving it untouched. Just as Stephen Blackpool is a worker infected with middle-class morality and therefore not a worker, so the heroes of *Absalom, Absalom!* and *Light in August* are not Negroes, but white men with a few drops of Negro blood.

I am talking about two novelists who 'loom large' in our literature, and that one should have been a snob and the other a racist is of no consequence, it will be said. But what I have

23 The superiority of Proust over James is due in part to the fact that Proust is Dickensian in his treatment of character; or, if he seeks to 'get closer', he seldom goes beyond *speculation*. James, on the contrary, fearlessly seats himself in the void, and because he gets so little resistance from his material the result is a convoluted and, in a sense, effortless triviality reminiscent of the seventeenth- and eighteenth-century novels of chivalry which also copied a purely invented reality and which also appealed to a class and a culture in decline.

been trying to show is that these men are important classical novelists *because* of their lamentable social attitudes, not *despite* them; that such attitudes are the 'logic' of identity, that a writer's personality is of less consequence than what he is permitted or inspired to say by the cultural structure of which he is a manifestation. Sartre has said it is unthinkable that a great novel be written in praise of anti-semitism; except, one might add, for the anti-semite himself who may well find no greatness elsewhere. The greatness of the classical novel will be unimpeachable for those least inclined to feel for its implicit content the abhorrence it deserves. Critics observe that there is no great working-class novel. How could there be? To be literate is to have learned the language of the White Destroyer; a language which, thanks to the separation of explanation and value, is almost always an alibi. To avoid using it Stendhal had to reinvent the novel and Jules Vallès—in exile—could only write a novel (the Jacques Vingras trilogy) which is in reality an autobiography.

We have been contrasting the work of Dickens as an 'object of knowledge' created by the professional appreciators for reasons best known to themselves, and that work as an experience, giving enormous satisfaction to a specific social class because Dickens provides reassurance of a quality to be found nowhere else. We can come back now to the problem mentioned at the beginning of the chapter: in what exactly consists the superiority of Dickens over the many *feuilletonistes* of his day? How can soap opera be genial? The answer must surely be sought in the direction of Dickens's humour; for whatever profundities (usually imaginary) the scholars may come upon in Dickens's fiction, coarser men read him for one reason only—he is wonderfully funny. However, since Dickens is the supreme spokesman of the middle class, it will be necessary to show that if Dickensian soap opera transcends itself through humour, then identity must be of the essence of such humour.

We saw that the evolution of the novel consisted largely in the gradual disappearance of the 'autonomous event'. In the classical novel things happen 'indirectly', through identity. This is the 'truth' of the novel, the 'necessity' at which the novelist aims. Because Dombey is *this kind of man,* certain

133

things 'inevitably' obtain (he will want a son to carry on the name, this will oblige him to remarry, he will be ruined not by the disruption of trade through war, or some such event, but by pride, etc.). All this applies to humour in Dickens but to an even greater degree; for humorous characters are those *entirely* independent of event. Ordinarily our interest in the story consists in wondering whether, or by what means, the event (the beyond) is going to confirm or invalidate our identifications; but for our satisfaction to be complete, the characters themselves must acquiesce in these identifications. In Dickens, consequently, the good and the bad always recognize themselves as such, otherwise the reader might entertain scruples as to the accuracy with which the beyond is fulfilling its role. The humorous characters, on the contrary, are those who are *mistaken about their identity*—supposing themselves to be of the elect, they in fact fall ludicrously short of it. Try to imagine Micawber with a perspective upon himself. It is unthinkable because what is funny is Micawber's conviction that he *is* a distinguished gentleman of great though unrecognized abilities, whereas the reader knows him *to be* (as an object *is*) hopelessly incapable and improvident. If Micawber were to avow that he had always known this he would cease instantly to be a comic character, just as would Sarah Gamp if she were to admit to being a venal old souse rather than a devoted public servant. But, one might object, Mrs. Gamp knows perfectly she is not a 'devoted public servant'—and here is the crux of the matter. Of course she would know this *in real life*, because in real life there is no identity, but in the novel she does not and *cannot* know it without ceasing to be one of Dickens's great comic creations. In the case of the good and evil character, the situation is the reverse; they must, as we saw a moment ago, have knowledge of their goodness or badness although once again, in real life, this never happens. We may admit that we acted badly on this or that occasion, but we do not suppose that we *are* bad unless, as is the case with many criminals, others succeed in forcing this identity upon us. The same, of course, applies to the 'good'. The notion that there exist good and evil people is partly the consequence of our refusal to admit the subjective evidence of an inner nothingness, an evidence we can endure only on condition of being freed from an obsessive awareness of the other; in other words, only upon the formation of a 'we', which will attain its goals in so far as each of us contributes not an identity but an effort.

There are a small number of characters in Dickens who straddle the lines. Pecksniff, for example, is both humorous and evil—humorous in so far as we see him playing piety while we know he is mean and unscrupulous; evil when at the end of the novel he is obliged by the assembled good characters to contemplate himself. Tigg, in the same novel, is an instructive case. He is in reality two separate persons. At first, Montagu Tigg, one of Dickens's funniest characters, an amiable sponger, who eventually becomes Tigg Montagu and loses most of his funniness because he acquires an identity of which he is aware (he becomes evil, a sort of prefiguration of Merdle, and is consequently murdered) having lost that about which he was 'mistaken'. The case of William Dorrit is a most interesting one. The problem may be expressed in this way: does a man presumably born a gentleman (correct accent, reasonable appearance, etc.) cease to be one as a result of twenty-five years' residence in a debtors' prison; and, if so, is this ontological endowment fully restored upon his acceding to wealth at the end of that period? We can answer unhesitatingly because in the same novel an indubitably good character (Clenham) also finds himself in the Marshalsea. Clenham reacts very differently from Dorrit; he begins at once to pine away; that is, as a good character he is *aware* that an imprisonment is an un-favourable pronouncement on the part of the beyond. How-ever, he refuses to help himself (accept Little Dorrit's money), the beyond realizes an error has been made and Clenham is released. Dorrit, on the contrary, refuses to be aware; he persists in mistaking his identity and is consequently a humorous character; though from time to time he is pathetic also, for he keeps approaching awareness.

The foregoing remarks may be summarized as follows: the novel, being about identity, is able to exploit an impossible ignorance of self (humour) and an equally impossible know-ledge (good and evil). In reality, the self, being act and not thing, can be neither known nor not known. In other words the cognitive attitude, appropriate for things, cannot be applied to man himself who must be thought of in terms of his goals.

We shall have to glance briefly at some of the great humorists who preceded Dickens, for this will help us to understand the exact nature of the transformation he brought about.

Humour in Dickens depends upon knowledge (of an identity) which is given to the reader but withheld from the character himself. There is consequently an inevitable element of condescension in our attitude toward these characters. It is inconceivable that we should ever be in any way *with them*, for they are closed up in an inner world of error, and since that error consists in their being mistaken about their identity they are necessarily independent of event, one of the purposes of which, as we saw, is to reveal identity to itself. Consequently, the difficulties we encounter in getting along with others, and which make up the greater part of pre-Dickensian humour, are largely done away with. It is not Micawber's relations with his creditors (which a Molière or a Fielding would have concentrated upon) which are funny, since they are very seldom directly presented, but his inability to see that he is in any way concerned—all this unpleasantness happens to someone whom he is not. Because the humorous characters in Dickens are manifestly and inexpugnably in error, they are condemned to be supernumeraries, whereas the great comic figures who preceded them either play the principal roles as in Cervantes and Molière, or come close to it as with Falstaff and Panurge. Only in *Don Quixote* is there an element of self-delusion; but this, of course, is in reality a touch of madness which, furthermore, develops into a kind of wisdom so that the Don, more often than not, is right to be wrong. He becomes the spokesman of what is best in us. Similarly, there is nothing negligible about Molière's great types; for however comically absurd their character, they stand firm against all comers with a fortitude and resourcefulness which from time to time excite our sympathy. Generally speaking the great comic creations before Dickens had weight; they are to be reckoned with, sometimes even on the intellectual level (Don Quixote, Panurge, Alceste). It is precisely in thinking about his humorous characters, however, that we are made most aware of how remote Dickens was from any suggestion of non-conformism in respect to the basic values of his society. Even when he is being explicit,

Dickens's revolutionary fervour does not really carry him beyond the recommendation that charity be made more efficient and humane; while implicitly, there is this fauna of quaint or laughable beings who not only do not question their society (the immemorial privilege of the 'fool'), they strive with all their might for its approval, the humour consisting in the discrepancy between the distinguished role they suppose themselves to be playing and the hopelessly inadequate spiritual and physical equipment of which they dispose. In the most purely comic characters the discrepancy is absolute (Micawber, Sarah Gamp, Mantalini, Turveydrop, etc.) and as it diminishes, the character becomes at once less comic and frequently more important to the plot. Newman Noggs, Major Bagstock, Flora Finching, had at least been at one time what they all too obviously are no longer—the first a country gentleman, the second a soldier, and the third a pretty young girl.

In broad terms, pre-Dickensian humour arises from the bizarre or unusual enterprises in which a man's character involves him (in contrast to the Dickensian character which is 'self-contained', the humour resulting from an unusual relationship with the self, rather than with others). To put this differently, we have the slowly developing bourgeois individual at odds with a culture which is still so solidly hierarchical that any attempt upon it can only be derisory; that is, in many circumstances, funny. (*Le Bourgeois Gentilhomme* is of course the model here.) But by the eighteenth century that same individual has become, in the name of Reason, so confident that his attacks cease to be comic and must be reckoned with on the philosophical plane. As a result, humour in the picaresque novel has far less to do with character; it comes to depend much more upon circumstance, so that interest no longer centres upon a curious non-conforming individual, but upon man's relations with the scheme of things. We have seen that the novel has always had to protect itself against triviality, so that the best picaresque fiction (a form not essentially concerned with scientific and/or ethical identification) usually carries a good charge of 'philosophy'. The novel, however, must tell a tale, it must be about existence; and yet before Marxism and existentialism any attempt to philosophize existence led to a didactico-moralistic literature for pious old maids. The only solution was to leaven one's philosophy with humour. In the best picaresque fiction this usually amounts to exploiting the comedy which can result from a dogmatic or unsupple application of philosophy to everyday life. *Candide* is consequently the purest example of the genre. *Tom Jones*, although of course a far greater book, belongs to the same family, with the role of Pangloss being taken by Thwackum and Square. At every turn Tom Jones violates the philosophies of either or both of these two persons, yet he is almost always right in so doing, while the reverse is true of the villain Blifil. The tavern brawls with which picaresque literature (including *Tom Jones*) is full are not in themselves funny, they become funny when they are used to illustrate the tenuousness of the link between ethical speculation and what may well happen. Character of course comes into this, but not indispensably as in Molière or Dickens. Fielding repeatedly reminds us that Tom Jones is a man like others; that is, neither good nor bad. It is characteristic of Tom Jones not to be able to resist a sexual invitation; but it is no fault of his that it should be Mrs. Waters of all people who was at that particular inn at just that moment.

Humour, or any other cultural phenomenon, does not have a definition which resists time, it has a significance or a function within a given social structure at this or that stage of its evolution. Picaresque humour, consequently, coming with the Enlightenment, conducts its own perverse meditation upon the Great Plan, and man's place within it.[24] Returning to Dickens, we can see that a very different kind of humour is introduced with *Pickwick*. It no longer has anything to do with speculation. As far as the now firmly established bourgeoisie is concerned the questions are answered once and for all, so that the novelist has a firm guide as to what kinds of people there are; and this,

24 The great comedy of the early part of the century (Chaplin, Harold Lloyd, Buster Keaton, etc.) is one which makes use of the fact that ours is a world where familiar things have a life of their own—they escape us. (This is one aspect of the 'alienation' of which Marx was the philosopher and Kafka the novelist.) The cinema was therefore essential to it since objects—like the teetering log cabin in *The Gold Rush*—can only be laughably animated by the various devices with which the cameraman produces his optical illusions.

as we have seen, comes to be what novels are really about. *Pickwick* remains superficially picaresque in that there is much aimless travelling about in the course of which funny things happen; but what is far more important, these things happen not by chance (as in the picaresque novel where they constitute an irreverent commentary upon an Order given to such lapses) but quite naturally since we are dealing with Sam Weller and the members of the Pickwick Club; that is, with people who are *by nature* and *in themselves* funny.

There is one other notable characteristic of Dickens's work—its sentimentalism—which we will deal with in conclusion. As with Dickens's humour, his sentimentalism will have to be made intelligible exclusively in terms of identity; not only because sentimentalism is so conspicuous in his novels, but because it would seem to be peculiar to our culture alone. We are always a little surprised to encounter it in eighteenth-century novels; in Dickens it is taken for granted.

Sentimentalism we all recognize at once, but we don't understand it, since empirical habits of thought exclude understanding. We know a lot about gravitation, we do not understand it (that is, we do not know *why* matter should have these characteristics rather than others), since there is no understanding without reference to purpose. The physical scientist not only can, but should, ignore teleology; to do this, however, in thinking about ourselves (and even, perhaps, about any living thing) is to accept a crippling handicap. We must, therefore, as always, ask what sentimentalism *does*, what do people mean by it?

Needless to say, sentimentalism is added to the facts, it does not reside there. Here is a passage from Reed's *Ten Days That Shook the World*: 'A couch lay along the wall, and on this was stretched a young workman. Two Red Guards were bending over him, the rest of the company did not pay any attention. In his breast was a hole; through his clothes fresh blood came welling up with every heart beat. His eyes were closed, and his young, bearded face was greenish white. Faintly and slowly he still breathed, with every breath sighing, "Mir boudit! Mir boudit!" (Peace is coming! Peace is coming!).' Reed made a note of what he saw, nothing more. His account is therefore devoid of sentimentalism. What is the difference between the death of this workman and that of little Nell? It is not that one is fact and the other fiction, since no one forced Dickens into his lachrymose organ effects and Reed could easily have sentimentalized. How could he have done so? We can answer at once because we know exactly how a Stalinist hack writing twenty years later would have described an event of this kind. His method would have been that of Dickens, consisting first in dwelling upon the workman *as such* (that is, any characteristic not attributable to his identity as a workman would have been ignored, just as Nell is the 'innocent young girl', not a concrete individual, but an abstraction) and then showing the connection between this disembodied idea of an individual and the beyond—historical law in one case, religion in the other. Reed was showing how revolutionary forces seized power in Russia, he was describing a praxis. We know exactly why the workman died, his was not a death that has to be 'explained away'. Sentimentalism, inversely, is the expression of gratitude that *human* ends should miraculously be achieved entirely *without recourse to a praxis*. It is the reaction of the individual, confined to the private realm and therefore *helpless*, to the announcement that there is a Meaning which renders effort and doubt superfluous. (Women are generally more sentimental than men because they are more helpless, they have a still greater need to believe that things really happen like that.)

The two basic characteristics of bourgeois culture with which we have directly or indirectly been concerned from the beginning emerge very clearly: first, the refusal to regard a praxis as in any way related to the 'objective' nature of things and second, the evolution of this attitude itself into a praxis which has proven supremely effective (witness the popularity of Dickens even in the old working class). It is indispensable to sentimentalism that the hero and heroine should receive their reward—either an apotheosis as in the case of Nell and Paul Dombey, or a 'happy ending'—not for what they *did*, but for what they *are*. The only exception I can recall to the absolute passivity of Dickens's good characters is Little Dorrit's momentary lapse, already mentioned, to be accounted for by the corrupting influence of the prison. Hence the interventions of

the beyond must be that much more frequent until, in the final
scenes, it all but appears in person to prove our fears ground-
less by demonstrating the perfect accord between our wishes
and the scheme of things; that is to say, by consecrating
identity.

Sentimentalism is quite simply the imbecility into which we
are led if we try to apply classical rationalism to everyday life.
We want desperately to believe that Order manifests itself, but
since we know it does not, we are usually a little ashamed of
being sentimental. Sentimentalism, however, insults not only
our intelligence, but our dignity. Reed's workman in a sense
willed his death by entertaining a revolutionary purpose;
and similarly the tragic hero engages in an action—in which
he risks his life—against whatever it is which is bent on his
destruction. Nell's death, on the contrary, is absurd unless she
can be shown ascending to receive her reward. If we ask
'reward for what?' we see at once why sentimentalism picks
on young women and children (exactly as did the factory
system)—they are rewarded for having *done nothing* in the
face of adversity, for having *accepted*. Such conduct always
degrades a man. *La Dame aux Camélias* was one of the greatest
sentimental triumphs of the century. In it the heroine proves
she is not really a whore since she is capable of 'true love';
an act by which, in effect, she begs to be readmitted to the
society which had cast her out. The interest of a sentimental
tale derives from the fact that the beyond seems to have made a
mistake in identity. But we know perfectly well that He who
marks the sparrow's fall is not going to suppose Nell to be the
improvident little slut she appears, nor is He going to suppose
that Paul Dombey resembles his old man. Paul, despite his
extreme youth, knows that 'money can't buy everything' and
so subscribes to our tenderest illusion about ourselves.

Sentimentalism, then, is the trusting submission to the
suprahuman; and consequently, by implication, the refusal
of solidarity with one's fellows. The sublime prototype of
tragedy is the story of Prometheus who, doomed to defeat,
nevertheless sided *with* men *against* the gods (Christ, it will be
recalled, though born of woman, made the opposite choice).
Given the bourgeois-rationalist view of the world, which
involves the separation of the public from the private realm, of

explanation from value, the choices are all negative. We can regard the beyond as benevolent, this being the choice of low-brow art and, ironically, of the Objective Society; we can regard it as indifferent or hostile, this is the choice of realism in all its forms; or, finally, we can try to wash our hands of the whole business, and this is aestheticism.

Conclusion

THE great achievement of contemporary anthropology is to have demonstrated that mankind is *one* in the sense that the impenetrability of one culture for another is due not to differences in 'mentality' but to the vastly different ways in which the real can be coherently structured. However 'primitive' a people may appear to be from *our* point of view, their world is always a coherent one; and the weirdness of their ways of thinking does not spring from a 'mind' (a scientific and philosophical use of what we have called identity) but from the manner in which they have organized their universe. It is this process of organization in all its forms, from manual labour to philosophy and art which is praxis and which is, as well, our 'common humanity'.

Incomprehension and hostility between peoples and individuals diminish where urgent, common tasks are thrust upon them; and what we have been studying in this book is a mentality which, at one and the same time, acknowledges these tasks and their urgency *and* makes it impossible for them to be honestly undertaken. This it achieves by divorcing the public and private realms so that one's only responsibility can safely be to the self, to one's 'quality as a person' since the public realm is that of anarchy and mob-violence or of natural law. But surely, we tend to think, it is a matter of the plainest common sense that our lives are determined by political and social conditions and that we must do something about them? There are few misconceptions more dangerous if we believe one of the nineteenth century's most fascinating documents for the light it throws upon the incredible confusion of liberal 'thinking' about this question.

Musset's *Lorenzaccio* deserves a far more detailed study than we have room for here. I shall content myself with the following remarks. We saw that the apparent or explicit subject of *Les Illusions Perdues* (Balzac's denunciation of the omnipotence of money) was not the 'real' subject, and similarly this play which would appear to be so clearly about politics, about the public

143

realm upon which the fate of all of us depends, is, in reality, a warning that any attempt to intervene in the public realm will not only be abortive, but one's good identity could be destroyed in the process. We are so conditioned as to take it quite for granted—even though one of Musset's main purposes was to revile the July Monarchy and to deliver himself of some important observations on the subject of democracy and tyranny—that the reader's interest should centre on Lorenzaccio *as an individual*; for his identity is skilfully kept in the balance (it is 'hidden') throughout the play. Just as the 'public realm' (Balzac's descriptions of literary and journalistic life in Paris) in *Les Illusions Perdues* exists to 'test' the character of Lucien de Rubempré, so Lorenzaccio kills the duke not to re-establish the Republic (which, the play makes clear, would be infinitely preferable to the tyranny of the Medicis) but to 'save his identity'.[1] *Lorenzaccio* sets forth in exemplary fashion the liberal's full awareness of our 'common humanity' (the necessity of combating tyranny, what we now call Fascism) along with his refusal or inability to quit the private realm; on grounds of 'morality' (identity) to be sure, but, more important, because at a deeper level, men are not worth it. As Musset has Lorenzaccio explain at great length (and Flaubert in particular will take up the refrain) the generality of mankind is beneath contempt, it gets what it deserves; let us not trouble ourselves about it. To find satisfaction in one's restriction to the private realm and to despise the 'masses' is one and the same thing. Since we are not dealing with ideas,

---

1 In rather the way architecture dominates the art of the middle ages, fiction dominates nineteenth-century art; so that drama as well as the novel is usually about identity as a given-proven. However, if the nineteenth-century theatre is of far less interest than the novel, it is because there is not enough 'room' in a play for an identity to be satisfactorily explored and proven. The result is a tendency towards melodrama; that is, an over-simplification of identity (good-evil) along with the sensationalism which follows from it. If *Lorenzaccio* is the nineteenth century's most successful play, one of the main reasons is that Musset created a hero who is in doubt about his own identity while the reader is not (Lorenzaccio's remorse, and especially his good intentions, indicate clearly that he is 'good'). This is exceedingly rare in the classical novel because it would conflict with the requirements of what we called showing, since the hero would have to be 'romantically' self-absorbed, somewhat in the manner of Constant's *Adolphe*.

but with a form of culture, it may not be sufficient to alter one's ideas. Hugo, in Sartre's *Les Mains Sales*, although he is revolted by the wealthy middle-class milieu into which he was born, remains nevertheless indelibly marked by it; for joining the communist party (altering his 'ideas') was simply a different manner of dealing with his *personal* problems. Hugo, like Lorenzaccio, is unable to break out of the stale confinement of the self or to overcome, again like Lorenzaccio, the resulting dislike of his fellow man; unable, in brief, to regard life as a series of tasks—and not as a state of being—so that passing judgments upon others, whether as individuals or in the mass, would no longer be pertinent.

The public figure *as such* (i.e., engaged in the actual work of government) is no concern of the classical novel. In *La Rabouilleuse*, for example, Balzac remarks of both Philippe Bridau and Maxence Gilet that they had qualities that might have made them great soldiers and statesmen.[2] But in their *private* lives (which must be decisive, since that is what the story is being told about) they are 'evil', and are punished accordingly. This, of course, is what we should have expected since nineteenth-century fiction is about what men *are*, not what they *do*, and in public life the latter cannot be easily ignored. Stendhal alone (since, as we saw, his novels are not about identity) is not obliged to leave politics to the explicit level which the reader can brush over rapidly so as to get on with the story.

We remarked that the classical novel could not be devoted to the public realm since that is the domain of the various historical and sociological 'sciences'. And while this is true, it is also true that the explicit level in fiction would never have existed had novelists been sure that matters of public concern could safely be left to scholars and scientists. So we are again,

2 Livre de Poche, 1960, pages 92 and 170. It is not unusual to find Balzac saying of a character (as he does of Max) that had he found himself in different circumstances he would have been a different person. We ought therefore to note that there is what we could call an 'innate' identity which is that of almost all major characters; and an identity which is, so to speak, 'in suspense' until it is 'triggered' by a certain environment. In this latter case identity remains of course a given; since whether it is received at birth, or later from the environment, it is *passively* received as a sort of 'stamp'.

as always, confronted by an inextricable combination of praxis and structural 'necessity'.

We can take it, nevertheless, that the public realm had, in a real sense, been abandoned by the men working with an art form which was that of the very culture whose political ideology proclaimed the right, and in fact the duty, of *every* man to concern himself about what was by definition a 'public thing', the republic. For such a sacrifice to have been practicable the novelist had to be convinced that in identity he had found a fixed, immutable, and hence readily observable reality. Since this is the cornerstone of my theory, I should like to enlarge upon a few points hoping to anticipate objections that might be raised.

It will be recalled first of all that my definition of the classical novel is also a norm for that novel; so that the nineteenth-century novelist was free to temper the merging of explanation and value in identity if he wished, but at the cost of somewhat disappointing the best critical opinion. It is difficult to attribute precise identities in a book like Maupassant's *Une Vie*, for example. They exist none the less in the sense that the reader will securely approve or disapprove of each character (he will approve almost without qualification of Jeanne and her parents and disapprove of her husband and son) a privilege he of course never enjoys in real life since no one is *universally* approved or disapproved of. So that in addition to the 'reification' of characters into victims (or, in Flaubert, victims or fools) realism after Balzac will usually make it possible for readers to *unanimously* separate the likeable from the objectionable.

It is to be expected that the identity of minor or secondary characters may sometimes be ambiguous since, after all, the story is not being told about them; they are kept at hand largely to be used as needed in throwing the hero's identity into clearer relief. Thus, in Balzac's *Un Début dans la Vie*, there is no doubt about Oscar Husson, the young man making his debut in life: he is mediocrity itself, *un homme ordinaire* as Balzac calls him; and this is 'proven' by having him make several ill-considered attempts to occupy a position in life to which his identity does not entitle him. (This novel is a sort of nineteenth-century *Bourgeois Gentilhomme*: it is no easier—in fact it is impossible—in the classical novel to change one's identity than it was in the seventeenth century for a commoner to become a noble.) In the case of Moreau, however, a secondary character, the reader does not have enough information to be absolutely sure. He has embezzled from his benefactor (but he could have taken far more than he did) and yet seems kind and generous, being the one reliable friend Madame Clapart has. Had Moreau been the hero of the novel, this uncertainty could not have persisted.

In *Ursule Mirouët*, once again, there can be no doubt about the heroine; as Balzac remarks: 'She was perfect'. But Minoret and Goupil, two lesser individuals, deserve mention because they might be considered to have 'changed'. Minoret does a very wrong thing indeed, but by the end of the novel he is leading an exemplary life. There is no difficulty here, however, because Minoret had been identified as 'stupid', not 'evil'; so that he is the same man throughout, but a very much chastened one eventually, having encountered in Ursule the Beyond personified.[3]

Goupil, on the other hand, is undoubtedly 'evil' at first, and yet we learn at the end that he is respected by the townspeople and is clearly leading the life of a 'good' man. In such instances what has happened is a too abrupt revelation of a hidden good identity; too abrupt because the novelist cannot be expected to focus the reader's full attention upon any more than one or two characters; and we are dealing *necessarily* with a hidden identity since one need only try to imagine a *series* of changes in a character in a classical novel to see that this cannot happen without the novel ceasing to 'tell'; or, to express this differently,

---

3 One would be justified in ignoring novels like *Ursule Mirouët* because, being full of Swedenborgian nonsense, they fail to 'show' adequately.

Let me recall that what I have tried to provide in this book is not the definition of a quintessential, Platonic Idea of a novel of which all existing novels (including *Ursule Mirouët*) would be a more or less satisfying approximation.

The novel *is* in so far as it *manifests* itself; and of these 'manifestations' the most important will be those which resolve most effectively the cultural dilemma of the nineteenth-century bourgeoisie. When the novelist becomes too 'individual' (Balzac's interest in Swedenborg) the result is not a work which partakes in its own way of the 'essence' of fiction, but one which is tiresome.

without the novel becoming a contemporary novel 'telling' that identity does not exist.

There is no need to continue. Balzac, of all nineteenth-century novelists, is the one whose work is richest in what might appear to be anomalies, or even exceptions to the theory I have put forward; in each case, however, a moment's examination will provide explanations like those just suggested.

In primitive societies the so-called rites of passage convert children into adults; and in the process they learn the 'secrets of the universe', so that when tools and weapons fail, other methods—prayer, magic—can be used to assure the tribe's survival. These rites are an awe-inspiring, unforgettable experience because the child has revealed to him nothing less than the reasons why the world is what it is. Being an adult is being able to *make sense* of things. The university is the 'rite of passage' in our society, but it does not inspire awe, nor is it unforgettable, [4] for the simple reason that our 'tools' having become all but omnipotent there is no further need for a *given* Meaning. And of course the university does not *name* one; it suggests rather that the student find it for himself or wait for it to appear. This is the comedy the student has come to find intolerable.

For the university teacher to be able to do his job properly he has to be able to show that there *is* meaning, but it is man-

---

4 Nor, might we add, does *everyone* participate as in primitive societies; in other words we exclude the majority of the population from any hope of acceding to the 'secrets'. Fortunately there are no secrets and the exclusion is simply from a more elaborate self-embellishment. The 'excluded', however, do not know this, and Fascism has a constant appeal because it places the 'secrets'—explanation in terms of 'kinds of people'—within reach of the most retarded. But these latter could not constitute a threat were they not abetted in one way or another by the whole society. The academic, for instance, not only 'waits', he has recourse continually to the 'kind of person' argument. In a recent edition of Engels's *Condition of the Working Class in England* (Oxford, 1958) we are informed by the editors that 'the fury with which Engels attacked the English middle classes in general and the factory owners in particular' was due 'at any rate to some extent' to 'an overwhelming sense of frustration'; and this presumably accounts for Engels's 'fundamental errors'. Marx also was perhaps 'frustrated'; for there was obviously no sound reason for his being so cross with the factory owners who, like our helpful editors, were simply doing their duty in the position to which it had pleased God to call them.

made; which is to say that it becomes clearer as we face up to the 'apodictic' tasks which *our particular* moment of history has placed before us; or, as Nietzsche put it: '. . . only he who is building up the future has a right to judge the past'.

Let me conclude then with a few words about what seems to me the relationship between the subject matter of the classical novel and the 'building up of the future'.[5]

The progress of our culture since Dickens has consisted in a vast clearing away of accumulated idols. Science long ago gave up pronouncing with any conviction upon the 'nature of the physical word', while the best of our literature and art has, since the turn of the century, been striving to unlearn our entire cultural past; and this is progress because the new is never difficult except in so far as we have been unable to rid ourselves of the old. On the other hand, this evolution has remained purely cultural, it has taken place within a still capitalistic society; one which, thanks to its immense productivity, has been able to provide its members with sufficient goods to transform them into a petty-bourgeoisie of 'individuals'. Marx, as we have seen, had already destroyed the idols (though scientific pseudo-Marxism had done its best to hush this up) by showing that human praxis is the ultimate source of all things. In the case of capitalism (hence Marx's hatred) the praxis is more or less deliberately concealed through recourse to a phoney religion and a phoney economics, and the role of the proletariat was to have demonstrated this irrefutably by changing the nature of an alleged 'objective' reality. This did not happen in any of the industrialized nations of the west. So we are in the position of knowing (if we know anything at all) that capitalism is the praxis of a given social group; of knowing, more generally, that reality as a whole can only be understood as the concretion of human purpose; and yet

5 If, despite all I have been able to say, the reader still considers that the novel can and should be studied in itself and that I have persistently strayed from the subject, let him reflect at least that, from the student's point of view (except, of course, for those who look forward to eventually replacing their teachers, in somewhat the way the educated African too often aspires to replace the departed white administrator) the humanities as now taught are 'off the subject' of the *life* he is going to lead.

we refuse to take the next step, to relinquish an individualism (meaningless apart from its opposite 'pole'—objective reality) which is a hidden praxis, so that there might emerge to full consciousness that 'we' which alone can rationalize a reality on the point of escaping altogether from our control.

Western capitalism was saved not only by a productivity which compelled it to raise the standard of living of its workers, but also on the 'ideological' level as a result of the fact that the revolution came first to an underdeveloped country. Marx had always maintained that one could not even begin to build socialism until there was enough of everything to go around (hence many of the bolsheviks believed that the revolution could not survive in Russia unless the workers seized power elsewhere in Europe—and in a sense it did not survive), otherwise the first task of the revolutionary government would be to cease being revolutionary in order to coerce its workers and peasants into providing the material base without which the new regime could not maintain itself in a capitalist world.

All this may be expressed more concisely as follows: what the Stalinists call bourgeois decadentism, in so far as it consists in the inability to subscribe to any of the time-worn verities, is progressive; but it is also impotent, for it is associated with an economy (and with the ideology of the Objective Society) which, by perpetuating the separation of the public and private realms, guarantees that thought shall remain an affair of the *individual*. Inversely, the communist underdeveloped countries could not possibly face their colossal tasks without a fusion of the public and private which, however, at the same time and as one aspect of the coercion just referred to, is saddled with a conservative ideology—that of scientific pseudo-Marxism.

The west may be counted upon to do everything it can to make coercion seem a permanent and inseparable component of communist power; but it will succeed only in causing the coercion to be more willingly accepted as the necessity for it is more apparent. Thus western hostility will reinforce precisely that element of communism—the fusion of public and private into a 'we'—which both makes it invulnerable and holds out the possibility that the day may come when, thanks to the abolition of want, coercion will shrink to an indispensable minimum, while the individual maintains his access to the public realm without which he can have neither real freedom nor real dignity.

The proletariat, as we remarked a moment ago, was to have proven that there is no fixed Reality but only this or that praxis with its particular goals. The twentieth-century communist revolutions have done just this, and the asininities of Stalinist dogma (which follow from the attempt to restore a fixed Reality—historical law) must eventually yield to this evidence—the non-human world of Realities-to-be-known which is that of classical rationalism, Stalinism and capitalism and which entails the reification of the self, vanishes at once when individuals coalesce into a community for which the Real is not essentially that which is learned (as in bourgeois rationalism) but that which is to be changed. Stalinism aims to obfuscate the true nature of Marxist revolution precisely as Napoleon tried to restore an aristocracy which the bourgeois revolution had destroyed. Stalinism therefore, like Bonapartism in its day, is a parasitical ideology; which does not mean that it must 'inevitably' be eclipsed when it is seen that the change in subject—I to we—has abolished 'objective' reality. But the possibility is there, and hence communism is progressive. In the west, on the contrary, despite the existence of an art far more progressive than socialist realism, despite the precious philosophical acquisitions of phenomenology and existentialism, an individualism (both philosophical and in the form of a 'fight for the private life', culture as *self-enrichment*) persists which, far from being called into question, is regarded as a bulwark against the 'dehumanization' of man. It is not the first time a civilization found a source of pride in the manner in which it dug its own grave.

Index

Index